LOW-CARB,

Slow & Easy

LOW-CARB,
Slow & Easy

Frances Towner Giedt

HPBooks

HP Books
Published by the Penguin Group
Penguin Group (USA) Inc.
375 Hudson Street, New York, New York 10014, USA
Penguin Group (Canada), 10 Alcorn Avenue, Toronto, Ontario M4V 3B2, Canada
(a division of Pearson Penguin Canada Inc.)
Penguin Books Ltd., 80 Strand, London WC2R 0RL, England
Penguin Group Ireland, 25 St. Stephen's Green, Dublin 2, Ireland (a division of Penguin Books Ltd.)
Penguin Group (Australia), 250 Camberwell Road, Camberwell, Victoria 3124, Australia
(a division of Pearson Australia Group Pty. Ltd.)
Penguin Books India Pvt. Ltd., 11 Community Centre, Panchsheel Park, New Delhi—110 017, India
Penguin Group (NZ), Cnr. Airborne and Rosedale Roads, Albany, Auckland 1310, New Zealand
(a division of Pearson New Zealand Ltd.)
Penguin Books (South Africa) (Pty.) Ltd., 24 Sturdee Avenue, Rosebank, Johannesburg 2196,
South Africa

Penguin Books Ltd., Registered Offices: 80 Strand, London WC2R 0RL, England

This book is an original publication of The Berkley Publishing Group.

Copyright © 2005 by Frances Towner Giedt
Cover design by Liz Sheehan

HP trade paperback edition: January 2005

Library of Congress Cataloging-in-Publication Data

Giedt, Frances Towner.
    Low-carb, slow & easy / Frances Towner Giedt.—1st Perigee pbk. ed.
        p.   cm.
    Includes index.
    ISBN 1-55788-451-X
    1. Low-carbohydrate diet—Recipes.   2. Electric cookery, Slow.   I. Title.

RM237.73.G453   2005
641.5'6383—dc22

                                                          2004053962

PRINTED IN THE UNITED STATES OF AMERICA

10   9   8   7   6   5   4   3   2   1

For Coleen O'Shea:
An agent who understands the cookbook business from
the inside out. It's always a pleasure to work with you.

Acknowledgments

MY FIRST THANKS go to my husband, David, who tirelessly cleaned up my messy kitchen after a day of testing, was endlessly supportive, and always willing to lift a fork to taste the end product of my many slow cookers. I am also grateful to John Duff, publisher of Perigee Books, for putting together another A-team to produce the finished project—his assistant, Kathryn McHugh; Jeanette Egan, editor; Charles Björklund, art director; Liz Sheehan, cover designer; Tiffany Estreicher, book interior designer; Kim Koren, managing editor; and Erica Rose, copy editor. I'm incredibly lucky to have all of you to guide this book through the publication process.

I'm also fortunate to have my personal support team of family and friends, who allowed me to pick their brains and draw from their culinary expertise. Your contributions of recipes are specifically noted within. And last but not least, my heartfelt thanks to my friend and agent, Coleen O'Shea, to whom I've dedicated this book, for guiding me through our eleventh cookbook project together.

Contents

Introduction
A Quick Review on Low-Carbing

I HAVE BEEN following a carb-counting regime since April 1970. That's when my obstetrician informed me that recent blood tests indicated that my body was no longer able to metabolize carbohydrates and that at twenty weeks pregnant, and without any history of diabetes in my family, I had developed gestational diabetes. I was advised by my doctors to severely restrict my carb intake, thereby lowering my blood glucose levels, to save my life and that of my unborn son. The diet worked and I delivered a healthy son, who today is in his early thirties. By the way, the diet I was given was in the form of two medical articles published in the *New England Journal of Medicine* by Robert C. Atkins, M.D., years before the publication of his first book, *Dr. Atkins' Diet Revolution* in 1973.

Some sixteen years later, carb-counting would again come into my life when I was again diagnosed as having diabetes, only this time there was no pregnancy and there would be no reversal of my inability to metabolize carbohydrates properly. In the years since, I have always been in tight control of my blood glucose levels, with my cholesterol and triglyceride levels well within ideal range. I have subsequently studied diabetes and worked with a writing partner who has type 1 diabetes, as well as with the world-famous Joslin Diabetes Center of Boston, to publish four definitive cookbooks for diabetics—*Gourmet, Quick and Easy, Healthy Carbohydrate,* and *Great Chefs Cook Healthy.* My partner and I also publish *Diabetic-*

Lifestyle, an online monthly magazine for people who are living with diabetes, which is accessed monthly by millions in this and 134 other countries.

When the American Diabetes Association (ADA) in 2000 decided that carb counting would become a recognized way to control diabetes, giving an alternative to the long-used exchange system, it was still considered that 60 percent of the day's calories should come from carbohydrates. As a person who would rather eat a potato than a piece of chocolate, a whole loaf of freshly baked peasant bread than a great steak, or a piece of fruit than most anything, I now know that I simply cannot metabolize 165 total grams of carbohydrate each day, which would be 60 percent of my 1,500-calorie diet. I gain weight quickly. At 100 total carbs a day, I can maintain weight, but at 80 grams or 60 grams, I feel even better and can actually lose one or two pounds a week, respectively.

Although the ADA has yet to come out in full support of a low-carb diet, they have now published their own reduced-carb cookbook. Recently, heart doctors have also started investigating low-carb diets for their patients. My own doctors at Baylor Heart Place in Dallas and at the Heart Center at Cleveland Clinic in Cleveland, Ohio, suggested to me that more closely following a lower-carb diet would be advisable. Little did they know that for years I've been doing just that. And I'm not alone—millions of people who have tried most every kind of diet imaginable have found hope and success with a low-carb or carb-counting diet.

If you are not already on a low-carb diet, check with your doctor before you start, as there may be a need to adjust any medications you are taking, especially when you start to lose weight. This is particularly true of people who have diabetes and are taking insulin, as the amount of insulin injected is in direct relation to the number of grams of carbohydrate they will be eating at a particular meal. People on oral diabetes medication may need less medication as their weight begins to drop. Doing self-testing of your blood glucose levels is crucial. While keeping a food diary may be boring, it can be a highly valuable diagnostic tool.

Remember, when you're counting carbs, every mouthful of food must be counted. Buy a pocket-size book on carb counting for foods that you'll be eating in addition to the recipes in this book. There are several good ones available at major bookstores.

What Is a Carb and What Do You Count?

A carbohydrate is one of the three basic food elements (the others are protein and fat). It's composed of carbon, hydrogen, and oxygen, and, contrary to what some people think, it's not just sugar. Carbohydrate is found in varying amounts in all foods except those that are totally protein and fat. Carbs are present in sugars, flours, starchy vegetables, fruit, milk products, and nonstarchy vegetables. They are even present in some shellfish such as clams, mussels, and tiger prawns.

Lest you think you can live just on foods that are high in protein, think again. Very high-protein diets will force your kidneys to work overtime. And we all know that an excessive amount of fat, especially saturated fat, which can come along with protein, can lead to all sorts of health problems. You'd be bored within a week on a protein-only diet and, once off your diet, scarfing mashed potatoes, white bread, and who knows what else. Some say to just keep away from the "whites"—white flour, white sugar, and white pasta. That doesn't really work, as fruits, vegetables, grains, legumes, and dairy products all have carbs, in addition to the dietary fiber and essential vitamins and minerals that are needed for good health, making them a healthier carb choice.

So, it comes down to choosing the right kind of carbs and making every gram of carbohydrate work for you. Simple carbohydrates—such as those in white bread, white potatoes, and sugary foods—will trigger a sudden dump of glucose into the bloodstream. That will give you a quick burst of energy followed by a crash as your blood sugar level drops once the sugars are absorbed. Opt instead for complex carbohydrates such as those found in whole grains and in some fruits and vegetables, which generate a slower, less intense, even rise in blood glucose levels.

Just remember, a carb is a carb, and every carb must be counted, or, like any diet where you cheat, this won't work. Those of you following a net carb diet, subtract the grams of dietary fiber from the grams of carbohydrate given in the nutritional analysis for each recipe. People with diabetes will count the total carbs (carb plus fiber) as the fiber amount has been counted in your daily carb allowance.

What About Salt?

WHEN YOU LOOK at the recipes, you will notice that only when it's needed do I call for a specific amount of salt. I have otherwise left the amount of salt used during cooking up to you. Many people, myself included, must limit their sodium intake each day because of medical conditions or medicines they are taking.

I personally use little or no salt in cooking. I do taste the food and add some if needed to bring out the flavors, but many dishes go to my table prepared entirely without salt. Other than one friend who reaches for the salt shaker before he even tastes the food, I've noticed that very few people feel their food needs salting.

Some foods, such as canned tomatoes and soy sauce, are high in sodium. Other than the diced variety, low-sodium canned tomatoes are difficult to find. I use reduced-sodium soy sauce. I also rely on herbs and spices for saltlike seasoning.

Nutritional Information

NUTRITIONAL INFORMATION AND diabetic exchanges are listed for each recipe using the latest data available from ESHA (The Food Processor, Version 8.2), the U.S. Department of Agriculture, and, when necessary, manufacturer's food labels. Grams of carbohydrate (including dietary fiber), grams of protein, grams of total fat, and calories are noted. If you're on a low-carb diet that counts net carbs, subtract the grams of dietary fiber from the total carbs. If you are following a diabetic carb-counting regime, you'll need to count the total carbs as your fiber has been calculated into your carb allowance.

Using a Slow Cooker

FOR OVER THIRTY YEARS, slow cookers have been available to ease the chore of getting meals on the table without spending hours in the kitchen. In today's busy world with two-income households, busy social schedules, and more families on the go, who has the time to cook? If you are on a low-carb diet or carb-counting regime, the dilemma of how to prepare a delicious low-carb meal without a lot of effort is even greater—most take-away and frozen dinners are not suitable for your diet.

Whether you wish to restrict carbohydrates a little or a lot, the recipes contained in this book can help. Not only are they easy to assemble and take virtually no care while they cook without further attention, these recipes are so delicious and satisfying that you'll find it easier to stick to your low-carb quest. If you have been using the grill to prepare your low-carb meals, before you start cooking low and slow, here are some tips to help you get the most from your slow cooker.

Different-Sized Slow Cookers

Slow cookers range in size from one to six quarts. Each recipe in this book specifies the minimum-size cooker that will accommodate the amount of ingredients called for. Check the capacity of your slow cookers to determine which one to use.

Variance in Cooking Times

With few exceptions I have given a range of cooking times, allowing for variances in slow cookers from manufacturer to manufacturer and climatic conditions (extreme humidity can affect cooking time). When cooking on LOW, you'll be cooking at 200°F, which is so low that exact timing is not crucial. Don't fret if you're delayed on the way home and the cooking time has been exceeded by a half hour or even an hour. It won't make much difference on most recipes cooked on LOW.

The HIGH setting is about 300°F, and the food will simmer and boil. At this heat level, the cooking time range is shorter and more crucial—when cooking on HIGH, food can be overcooked, especially poultry. It is not recommended that you use the HIGH setting if you're going to be away from home. You can always start a recipe on LOW and, when you return home, finish it on HIGH.

Don't be tempted to lift the lid and peek into the slow cooker, as precious steam will escape. It's this hot steam that's cooking the food, and even a quick lifting of the lid can add an additional 20 minutes to the cooking time in order to raise the heat back to its desired temperature. Most foods do not require stirring during the cooking time. In those recipes where I've instructed you to stir, add an ingredient, or remove the lid, those extra minutes have already been figured into the total cooking time.

I suggest that the first time you use a recipe, note the time needed by your slow cooker for future use, especially if you live in a high-altitude area where you already extend cooking times.

Keep Food Safe

At the LOW setting, a slow cooker will be above 180°F, the temperature at which any possible bacteria in the food will be killed. Once cooked, it's essential that you keep food safe by keeping the cooker plugged in on LOW until the food has been served (the cooker can go right to the table). If you are taking the unit away from home you can purchase a special thermal cover from the Rival Manufacturing

Company that will fit most units, or you can wrap the slow cooker with the lid in place in two layers of foil, and then at least six layers of newspaper. Secure the wrapping with tape. Then place the wrapped unit upright in a large paper bag or box. Don't unwrap the unit until you're ready to serve.

Remove any leftovers promptly and refrigerate or freeze in proper storage containers. The food will not be chilled quickly enough if you place the crockery insert with the food inside in the refrigerator after cooking. Use any refrigerated leftovers within a day or two, and frozen leftovers within two months.

Further Reducing the Fat

Although I've called for very little added fat, and then mostly good fat in the form of olive or canola oil, you can further reduce the fat of a finished dish by choosing lean cuts of meat and trimming away as much visible fat as possible. When cooking poultry, remove the skin and as much visible fat as possible. When browning meat or poultry, you can further reduce the fat by using a cooking spray instead of the oil called for in the recipe. Skim the fat from the surface of the cooking liquid before using.

Let's Get Started

It's time to dust off your crockery slow cooker—or invest in a new cooker or two, maybe one of the new programmable models that will automatically start your cooking while you're involved elsewhere. Slow cooking can save you lots of time in the kitchen; it's almost like having your personal chef at home, cooking your dinner (or most of it) while you're busy doing other things.

I have given you a variety of delectable recipes, from party appetizers to savory soups, stews, and chili, to mouthwatering entrees that are meltingly tender, go-with vegetables, and a few desserts—all within your low-carb or carb-counting dietary needs. About the only food missed is fish, which with the exception of soups and stews, is better cooked on the grill, on top of the stove, and in the oven or microwave.

Savory Hot Dips and Appetizers

IF YOU'RE ON A low-carb diet, you'll be restricting your appetizers to party time. Often when we're busy and caught up in just getting a meal on the table or just getting the house ready for company, we opt for crudités and dip. As great as that is for dieters, there are times when we want to "pull out all the stops" and prepare something fantastic.

The slow cooker can help you create enticing appetizers that are wonderfully easy to make. Fancy luscious Caponata, a dish that requires constant attention when made on the stove? Who could resist a spicy chicken wing to dip in a cooling raita or an Asian-spiced pork rib to nibble on? My savory appetizer cheesecake made with goat cheese is delightful spooned onto a crisp Belgian endive leaf. Mexican Meatballs in Salsa and Hot Time Party Franks are super when you're entertaining a crowd. And who could resist a few of the Texas Party Pecans? Not me! Throw in the several recipes for savory hot dips and you're ready to throw a party. So, call up some friends and enjoy!

South-of-the-Border Cheese Fondue with Cauliflower Dippers

When Mike Roy, veteran of "Mike Roy's Kitchen" cooking show for over twenty years on CBS Radio, wrote his crockery cookbook, I fixed this fondue to serve with cubed French bread for a press party I hosted around my Southern California swimming pool and orchard. I've updated his recipe with fresh chiles and serve it with small florets of raw cauliflower for low-carb dipping, speared by long fondue forks.

Mark each fork with the person's name so there's no confusion. If you don't have enough fondue forks for everyone, I bet friends would be willing to loan you theirs—as long as they are invited to the party. In a pinch, use round wooden skewers.

This recipe produces a smoother dip when it's cooked only on the LOW temperature setting.

MAKES 10 SERVINGS

1 pound sharp cheddar cheese, cubed
1 pound Monterey Jack cheese, cubed
1 medium tomato, peeled, seeded, and diced
3 Anaheim chiles, seeded and finely diced
1 to 2 jalapeño chiles, seeded and minced
1 (1.2-ounce) package taco seasoning mix
Raw cauliflower florets, for dipping

Combine all the ingredients *except* the cauliflower in a 3-quart slow cooker. Cover and cook on LOW for 2 to 3 hours. Stir well until the ingredients are combined. Keep the cooker on LOW for serving. Surround with small cauliflower florets, allowing 6 to 7 pieces per person.

○ PER SERVING (DIP ONLY): 5 g carbohydrate, 21 g protein, 30 g fat, 254 calories
○ DIABETIC EXCHANGES: 1 vegetable, 3 lean protein, 4 fat

Bacon-Chipotle Cheese Dip

**MAKES ABOUT 10 CUPS;
40 SERVINGS**

2 (8-ounce) packages cream
    cheese, at room
    temperature, cut into small
    pieces
2 cups shredded Monterey Jack
    cheese
2 cups shredded cheddar cheese
2 cups sour cream
3 to 4 canned chipotle chiles in
    adobo sauce, minced
1 cup thinly sliced green
    onions, including some
    green tops
1 tablespoon Worcestershire
    sauce
1/2 teaspoon freshly ground
    pepper
6 strips bacon, crisply cooked
    and crumbled (about 1/2 cup)
Broccoli florets and toasted
    whole-wheat pita wedges,
    for dipping

This is sure to be a hit at your next party. For yourself and others counting carbs, offer small raw broccoli florets for dipping and, for those with carbs to spare, toasted whole-wheat pita wedges.

This recipe is not recommended for HIGH temperature cooking.

In a 3½-quart or larger crockery slow cooker, combine the cream cheese, Monterey Jack cheese, cheddar cheese, sour cream, chipotle chiles, green onions, Worcestershire sauce, and pepper.

Cover and cook on LOW for 4 to 5 hours. Whisk to combine, and stir in the bacon. Keep warm on LOW heat setting for 1 to 2 hours. Serve warm with broccoli florets and pita wedges.

○ PER 1/4-CUP SERVING (DIP ONLY): 1 g carbohydrate (includes trace dietary fiber), 4 g protein, 10 g fat, 114 calories
○ DIABETIC EXCHANGES: 1/2 lean meat, 1 1/2 fat

Hot Spinach-Artichoke Dip

Tote this one to your next tailgate party. Rival, the Crock-Pot® company, sells an insulated carrier for slow cookers, or you can wrap the crock insert in several layers of newspaper and then wrap it in a heavy beach towel. This'll keep the insert and contents warm until you arrive. Once there, the dip will disappear so quickly that keeping it warm won't matter.

Either Parmesan or Romano cheese may be substituted for the Asiago cheese with good results. If you're going to be using pita wedges for dippers, be sure to count your carbs carefully! This recipe is not recommended for HIGH temperature cooking.

In a 3½-quart or larger crockery slow cooker, combine all the ingredients *except* the vegetables for dipping.

Cover and cook on LOW for 3 to 4 hours. Keep warm on LOW heat setting for 1 hour. Serve warm with veggies or pita wedges.

○ PER ¼-CUP SERVING (DIP ONLY): 5 g carbohydrate (includes 1 g dietary fiber), 5 g protein, 12 g fat, 144 calories
○ DIABETIC EXCHANGES: 1 vegetable, ½ lean meat, 2 fat

**MAKES ABOUT 8 CUPS;
24 SERVINGS**

2 (8-ounce) packages cream cheese, softened and cut into pieces

2 (14-ounce) cans artichoke hearts, drained and coarsely chopped

1 cup chopped frozen spinach, thawed and squeezed dry

2 medium leeks, white and pale green parts, chopped

½ cup mayonnaise

1 teaspoon crushed dried Italian herb seasoning

¼ teaspoon garlic salt

1 cup shredded Asiago cheese

½ cup shredded mozzarella cheese

Raw cut-up vegetables or toasted whole-wheat pita wedges, for dipping

CRUDITÉS

Crudités (cut up raw vegetables) play an important role in a low-carb diet. In addition to being filling, they carry few grams of carbohydrate and a substantial amount of dietary fiber, a form of carbohydrate essential to good health.

Use these raw or barely blanched vegetables freely:

Asparagus (4 grams per 8 spears)

Beans, snap or green (4 grams per 1/2 cup)

Broccoli (5 grams per 1 cup)

Carrots, mini (5 grams per 8 pieces)

Cauliflower (5 grams per 1 cup)

Celery (4 grams per 1 cup)

Cucumber (3 grams per 1 cup)

Mushrooms (4 grams per 1 cup)

Pea pods (5 grams per 1/2 cup)

Squash, summer (5 grams per 1 cup)

Sweet bell peppers (5 grams per medium pepper)

Tomatoes, cherry (5 grams per 6 pieces)

Turnips (4 grams per 1/2 cup)

Zucchini (4 grams per 1 cup)

Bagna Cauda

A hearty Italian dip for fresh vegetables, Bagna Cauda was very popular at parties in the 1960s and '70s, only to be pushed aside when we were all told to reduce fat grams in our diet. Happily, the recipe can be resurrected in light of today's lower carb diets, where we're not so concerned about fat intake. A slow cooker is great for preparing and serving this yummy, garlicky dip for crisp, raw vegetables. Allow 6 to 7 pieces of raw vegetables per 5 grams of carbohydrate or 1 vegetable exchange.

This recipe is not recommended for HIGH temperature cooking.

In a 2½-quart crockery slow cooker, combine all the ingredients *except* the vegetables for dipping. Cover and cook on LOW until the butter has melted, about 1 hour.

Stir well and surround with vegetables for dipping.

○ PER SERVING (DIP ONLY): 1 g carbohydrate (includes trace dietary fiber), 2 g protein, 27 g fat, 254 calories
○ DIABETIC EXCHANGES: 5¹/₂ fat

MAKES 16 SERVINGS

1¹/₂ cups extra-virgin olive oil
¹/₂ cup (1 stick) unsalted butter
2 (2-ounce) cans anchovy fillets, drained, rinsed, drained again, and mashed to a paste
12 cloves garlic, thinly sliced
Fresh vegetables for dipping— choose 4 or 5 from the following: small radicchio leaves, Belgian endive leaves, pieces of red and yellow bell peppers, baby carrots, small cauliflower or broccoli florets, small mushrooms, slices of zucchini, slices of fresh fennel

Hot Crab Dip

MAKES 12 SERVINGS

12 ounces cream cheese, diced

¹/₄ cup heavy cream

2 (6¹/₂-ounce) cans lump
  crabmeat, picked over and
  flaked

¹/₃ cup grated onion

3 tablespoons mayonnaise

1 tablespoon prepared horseradish, drained

1¹/₂ teaspoons Tabasco sauce, or
  to taste

¹/₂ teaspoon dry mustard

1 tablespoon fresh lemon juice

Salt and freshly ground pepper,
  to taste

¹/₃ cup sliced almonds, toasted

2 tablespoons minced fresh
  parsley

Celery sticks, for dipping

*This is a party favorite at my house. Not only does the dip cook effort-
lessly without much attention, it also keeps at the right serving temperature on the buffet table. That's my kind of party recipe!*

In a 1-quart crockery slow cooker, combine the cream cheese
and heavy cream. Cover and cook on HIGH until the cheese
melts, about 45 minutes. Add the crab, onion, mayonnaise,
horseradish, Tabasco sauce, and dry mustard, and stir thoroughly.
Cover and continue to cook on HIGH for another 30 minutes.

Reduce the cooking temperature to LOW and stir in the
lemon juice. Taste and add salt and pepper as needed. Sprinkle
with the almonds and parsley. Position the cooker for serving.
Offer a basket of celery sticks for dipping.

○ PER ¹/₄-CUP SERVING (DIP ONLY): 2 g carbohydrate (includes trace dietary fiber), 7 g protein, 16 g fat, 180 calories

○ DIABETIC EXCHANGES: ¹/₂ very lean meat, ¹/₂ lean meat, 3 fat

Asian Appetizer Ribs

Hoisin sauce adds an intense Asian flavor to these finger-licking ribs, which are sure to be a hit at your next garden party. Supply plenty of paper cocktail napkins. Have your butcher cut the rack in half lengthwise for appetizer portions.

Preheat the broiler.

Rub the spareribs with salt and pepper and broil for 15 minutes, turning once, until the ribs are nicely browned. Transfer the ribs to a 3½-quart or larger crockery slow cooker. Combine the remaining ingredients in a bowl and pour over the ribs.

Cover and cook on LOW for 8 to 10 hours or on HIGH for 4 to 5 hours. Serve hot from the slow cooker set on LOW.

○ PER SERVING: 3 g carbohydrate (includes trace dietary fiber), 9 g protein, 13 g fat, 164 calories
○ DIABETIC EXCHANGES: 1 lean meat, 2 fat

MAKES 12 SERVINGS

1 (2¼- to 2½-pound) rack pork back ribs, fat rimmed and cut into separate ribs (see recipe headnote)

Salt and freshly ground pepper, to taste

¼ cup minced scallions

2 cloves garlic, minced

1 tablespoon grated fresh ginger

½ cup reduced-sodium soy sauce

2 tablespoons dry sherry

2 tablespoons hoisin sauce

2 tablespoons fresh lime juice

1 teaspoon Chinese five-spice powder

Savory Goat Cheese Cheesecake au Poivre

MAKES 24 SERVINGS

1 tablespoon unsalted butter, softened

6 ounces pecan halves, toasted and finely chopped

2 (8-ounce) packages cream cheese, at room temperature

8 ounces fresh goat cheese, at room temperature

2 large eggs, at room temperature

½ cup sour cream plus ¼ cup for garnish

1 teaspoon Dijon mustard

1 tablespoon cornstarch

Freshly ground pepper, to taste

I can drive an hour round-trip by freeway to Fort Worth and buy a similar appetizer cheesecake from a popular gourmet take-away food shop for $24. Because it takes only minutes to assemble, I'd rather shop locally for wonderful goat cheese from the Texas Hill Country and "bake" the cheesecake in my slow cooker for a fraction of the cost in time and money. At your market, look for a mild goat cheese such as Bucheron or Montrachet. You can make this up to 2 days ahead; it needs to chill for at least 4 hours and stand at room temperature for 1 hour before serving.

Serve this on your prettiest platter, surrounded with leaves of Belgian endive and crisp low-carb crackers for spreading. The recipe is not appropriate for cooking on LOW.

Spread the butter on the bottom and sides of an 8-inch round springform pan. Press the pecans onto the bottom of the pan.

In a large bowl and using a hand-held mixer on medium speed, beat the cream cheese until smooth. Gradually beat in the goat cheese, beating until smooth. Beat in the eggs, the ½ cup sour cream, Dijon mustard, and cornstarch. Spread evenly in the prepared pan.

Pour 2 cups hot water into a 5-quart or larger crockery slow cooker. Place the pan in the slow cooker (the water should come about 1 inch up the sides of the pan). Cover and cook on HIGH for 2½ to 3 hours, until the sides of the cheesecake have risen. Turn the cooker off and let stand, uncovered, until the pan is cool enough to handle. Remove the pan from the cooker.

Cover and refrigerate for at least 4 hours or up to 2 days. Run a sharp knife around the inside of the pan to loosen the cheesecake. Remove the sides, leaving the cheesecake on the removable bottom. Bring the cheesecake to room temperature, about 1 hour. Just before serving, spread the remaining ¼ cup sour cream on the top and sprinkle generously with pepper.

O PER ¼-CUP SERVING: 2 g carbohydrate (includes 1 g dietary fiber), 5 g protein, 16 g fat, 166 calories
O DIABETIC EXCHANGES: ½ lean meat, 2½ fat

Caponata

**MAKES ABOUT 6 CUPS;
24 SERVINGS**

1 (about 1¼-pound) eggplant,
  unpeeled, cut into 1-inch
  cubes
1 teaspoon salt, plus addtional
  as needed
1 cup chopped fennel
1 cup chopped onion
1 cup chopped red bell pepper
2 medium zucchini, cut into ½-
  inch cubes
2 cloves garlic, minced
1 (14½-ounce) can peeled
  Italian tomatoes
2 tablespoons extra-virgin olive
  oil
2 tablespoons tomato paste
2 tablespoons red wine vinegar
1 tablespoon Splenda sugar
  substitute
1 teaspoon crushed dried basil
¼ teaspoon crushed red pepper
  flakes
2 tablespoons capers, rinsed
  and drained
⅓ cup black imported olives,
  such as kalamata, pitted and
  chopped

This is a wonderful appetizer—a staple on most Italian cold antipasto platters. You can make this on top of the stove, but it needs to be watched carefully and stirred to prevent scorching. In a slow-cooker, caponata cooks to perfection without constant attention. Plan ahead, as it needs to be made at least the day before serving to allow the flavors to mellow. It will keep in the refrigerator for a week or freeze for up to 1 month.

Sprinkle the eggplant with the 1 teaspoon salt and place in a large colander. Set the colander over a large bowl and allow the eggplant to drain for 1 hour. Rinse the eggplant under cold running water to wash off the salt and drain well. Place the eggplant in the bottom of a 3½-quart or larger crockery slow cooker. Top with the fennel, onion, bell pepper, zucchini, and garlic. Do not stir.

Drain the tomatoes, discarding all but ¼ cup of the juice. Chop the tomatoes and add to the slow cooker. In a large measuring cup, combine the reserved tomato juice, olive oil, tomato paste, vinegar, Splenda, basil, and red pepper flakes. Whisk to combine thoroughly. Pour over the vegetables.

Cover and cook on LOW for 6 hours. Uncover and increase the cooking temperature to HIGH. Continue to cook until the excess liquid evaporates and the vegetables are very tender, 30 to 40 minutes. Transfer the mixture to a container and allow to cool to room temperature. Stir in the capers and olives. Taste and add salt, if needed. Cover and refrigerate overnight. Return to room temperature before serving.

○ PER ¼-CUP SERVING: 3 g carbohydrate (includes 1 g dietary fiber), 1 g
  protein, 1 g total fat, 28 calories
○ DIABETIC EXCHANGES: ½ vegetable

Indian-Spiced Chicken Wings with Tomato-Cucumber Raita

Chicken wings are always popular at parties, so make plenty. These wings are a bit spicy; the raita alongside is a welcome cooling counterpoint. This recipe fits nicely in a 3½-quart slow cooker. When using a 5-quart or larger cooker, double the recipe. Be sure to provide plenty of napkins.

MAKES 32 WING SECTIONS;
16 APPETIZER SERVINGS

16 large chicken wings (about 3
　　pounds total)
Salt and freshly ground pepper,
　　to taste
4 tablespoons (½ stick)
　　unsalted butter, cut into bits
¼ cup canned low-sodium
　　chicken broth
¼ cup minced scallions (white
　　part and 2 inches green)
¼ cup minced fresh cilantro
1 tablespoon curry powder
1 teaspoon ground cumin
1 teaspoon ground coriander
½ teaspoon ground cardamom

Tomato-Cucumber Raita (see
　　page 18)

Preheat the broiler.

Cut off and discard the wing tips. Divide each wing into 2 sections by cutting at the joint. Rinse the chicken and pat dry. Season with salt and pepper. Place the wings on a broiler pan and broil for 5 to 6 minutes per side, until the chicken is browned, turning once. Transfer the wings to a 3½-quart or larger crockery slow cooker.

In a small saucepan, melt the butter over medium heat. Add the remaining ingredients *except* the tomato–cucumber raita. Cook, stirring, until the butter mixture is fragrant, about 3 minutes. Pour over the chicken wings.

Cover and cook on LOW 5 to 6 hours or on HIGH for 2 to 3 hours. Serve the hot wings from the cooker with a bowl of the raita alongside for dipping.

○ **PER SERVING (CHICKEN ONLY):** trace carbohydrate (includes trace dietary fiber), 9 g protein, 9 g fat, 125 calories
○ **DIABETIC EXCHANGES:** 1 lean meat, 1 fat

Tomato-Cucumber Raita

MAKES ABOUT 2½ CUPS

1 large plum tomato, halved,
     seeded, and finely diced
1 medium cucumber, halved,
     seeded, and coarsely
     shredded
¼ teaspoon coarse salt
2 cups plain low-fat yogurt
1 serrano chile, seeded and
     finely minced
1 clove garlic, minced
1 tablespoon fresh lemon juice
¼ teaspoon ground cumin
2 tablespoons minced fresh
     cilantro

Place the tomato and cucumber in a fine strainer set over a bowl. Sprinkle with the salt and let stand for 30 minutes to drain. Meanwhile, place the yogurt in another strainer lined with a paper coffee filter. Set over a bowl and let stand for 30 minutes to drain.

Transfer the drained tomato-cucumber mixture and the drained yogurt to a mixing bowl. Stir in the chile, garlic, lemon juice, cumin, and cilantro. Cover and refrigerate for up to 2 days. When ready to serve, transfer the raita to a serving dish for dipping.

○ **PER 2-TABLESPOON SERVING:** 6 g carbohydrate (includes trace dietary fiber), 4 g protein, 1 g total fat, 53 calories
○ **DIABETIC EXCHANGES:** ½ skim milk

Mexican Meatballs in Salsa

Years ago, a friend brought a slow cooker full of these fabulous meat-balls to a party I was giving. They went quickly, and the recipe is still one of my party favorites. Once you've added the sour cream, keep the temperature setting on LOW to keep the sauce smooth.

Preheat the oven to 500°F.

Heat the oil in a large nonstick skillet over medium heat. Add the onion, garlic, and bell pepper. Sauté until the vegetables are limp, about 4 minutes. Transfer to a large bowl and combine with the ground beef, croutons, eggs, chili powder, oregano, paprika, salt, thyme, cumin, and pepper. Using your hands, gradually mix in the cheese. Form the mixture into 1-inch balls and place on a baking sheet. Bake for 5 minutes. Remove from the oven and drain well.

Place the browned meatballs in a 3½-quart or larger crockery slow cooker. Spoon the salsa over the meatballs.

Cover and cook on HIGH for 2 to 3 hours. Lower the temperature setting to LOW and gently stir in the sour cream and cilantro. Keep warm on the LOW temperature setting for up to 2 hours. Use wooden toothpicks to serve.

○ PER 4-MEATBALL SERVING: 4 g carbohydrate (includes 1 g dietary fiber), 16 g protein, 4 g fat, 152 calories
○ DIABETIC EXCHANGES: ½ vegetable, 2 very lean meat, 1 fat

MAKES ABOUT 80 MEATBALLS;
20 SERVINGS

2 teaspoons extra-virgin olive oil
1 medium onion, chopped
2 cloves garlic, minced
1 medium red bell pepper, seeded and minced
3 pounds ground beef sirloin
½ cup garlic croutons, smashed
2 large eggs, lightly beaten
1 teaspoon chili powder
1 teaspoon crushed dried oregano
½ teaspoon sweet paprika
½ teaspoon salt
½ teaspoon crushed dried thyme
¼ teaspoon ground cumin
¼ teaspoon freshly ground pepper
1 cup shredded Monterey Jack cheese
1 (16-ounce) jar hot or mild salsa
1 cup sour cream
¼ cup minced fresh cilantro

Hot Time Party Franks

MAKES 16 SERVINGS

1 (16-ounce) package cocktail
  franks or smoked sausage
  links
1 cup tomato-based chili sauce
1 small onion, grated
½ cup sugar-free apricot
  preserves
2 canned chipotle chiles in
  adobo sauce, minced

Add some zip to your usual party fare with this updated version of cocktail franks. To keep the carb count as low as possible, be sure to use sugar-free preserves.

In a 1½-quart crockery slow cooker, combine all ingredients. Cover and cook on LOW for 4 hours. Serve hot from the slow cooker with wooden toothpicks.

O **PER 3-FRANK SERVING:** 7 g carbohydrate (includes trace dietary fiber), 4 g protein, 7 g fat, 106 calories
O **DIABETIC EXCHANGES:** ½ lean meat, 1 fat

Texas Party Pecans

Pecan trees grow everywhere here in Texas—both as an ornamental tree in neighbors' yards and as a cash crop. I buy shelled pecans in bulk from a roadside stand just prior to the holiday season when they are the cheapest and put bags of them in the freezer. This is just one of their many uses—a healthy appetizer that I can throw into my slow cooker. They are gently toasted to their best flavor without any possibility of scorching. Packed into glass jars and tied with a length of raffia, these pecans make great hostess gifts.

In a 3½-quart crockery slow cooker, combine all ingredients. Cover and cook on HIGH for 15 minutes. Reduce the heat to LOW, uncover, and cook for 2 hours, stirring occasionally. Spread the pecans on a parchment paper–lined baking sheet and cool completely before serving or storing in airtight containers.

MAKES ABOUT 4 CUPS; 16 SERVINGS

4 cups shelled pecan halves
¼ cup (½ stick) unsalted butter, melted
1 teaspoon ground cumin
1 teaspoon crushed dried thyme
1 teaspoon coarse salt
½ teaspoon cayenne pepper
½ teaspoon freshly ground pepper
½ teaspoon ground nutmeg

○ PER ¼-CUP SERVING: 4 g carbohydrate (includes 3 g dietary fiber), 3 g protein, 22 g fat, 212 calories
○ DIABETIC EXCHANGES: 4 fat

NOTE:

Pecans will appear soft after cooking but will crisp as they cool. If cooking in a larger slow cooker, you will need to double or triple the recipe so the slow cooker is at least half full with the nut mixture.

NUTS IN A LOW-CARB DIET

Forbidden in most diets because of their high-fat content, nuts can be a part of your low-carb regime. At only 5 grams of carbohydrate per ¼ cup, nuts are protein-rich and very good for you. Nuts are full of essential minerals such as calcium, phosphorus, magnesium, potassium, vitamin E, antioxidants, and good dietary fats. Some studies show that the good fat in nuts helps the body to metabolize fats and balance the HDL and LDL cholesterol, as well as break down the harmful fats surrounding the heart and liver.

Soups, Stews, and Chilies

THERE'S NOTHING MORE COMFORTING or inviting on a day when you're weary from work or play than a bowl of hot soup, stew, or chili. Complete by itself, no more is required than a fresh salad and a simple dessert to make a meal special enough for company.

When everyone in your family is on a different schedule, soup or stew is your answer as to what to serve. It cooks unattended all day, and everyone can serve themselves when it's time for supper. The recipes here are a versatile bunch. You'll find hearty soups like my Better Than Mom's Chicken Soup, Chipotle Steak and Shiitake Mushroom Soup, or Hearty Mediterranean Fish Soup. If you just want to serve a cup or small bowl of soup as a first course, pick from Curried Cream of Cauliflower and Apple Soup, Roasted Garlic Soup, or Savory Cream of Tomato Soup, among others. When we lived in Connecticut and my sons were active in soccer and lacrosse, stew such as Dixie-Style Chicken Stew, Parvine's Beef Stew, or Curried Pork Stew waiting back at home in the slow cooker saved me lots of time when we'd arrive home and everyone was starving and could hardly wait to sit down to a warm, filling meal. Chili is a matter of some controversy—some argue that the all-American "bowl of red" must have beans; others say it must not have tomatoes. I've offered a variety of chili recipes that have served me well over the years and will satisfy most every chili lover. All benefit from the slow, low heat of a crockery slow cooker.

Better Than Mom's Chicken Soup

Reminiscent of the soup my mom used to make when I had a cold or was chilled to the bone from the frigid Kansas wind, this dish is easy to put together.

Rinse the chicken pieces; remove and discard all the skin and fat, leaving the bones intact. Set aside. Place the onions in the bottom of a 3½-quart or larger slow cooker. Arrange the chicken pieces on top and cover with the tomatoes and juice, chicken broth, lemon juice, Italian seasoning, paprika, garlic powder, and bay leaves. Cover and cook on LOW for 5 hours, until the chicken is cooked and falling off the bones.

Taste and add salt and pepper, if desired. Add the pasta and raise the heat to HIGH. Cover and cook until pasta is tender, about 15 minutes. Ladle into shallow soup bowls and serve.

○ PER SERVING: 28 g carbohydrate (includes 3 g fiber), 38 g protein, 15 g fat, 395 calories

○ DIABETIC EXCHANGES: 1 bread/starch, 2 vegetable, 4½ very lean meat

MAKES 6 SERVINGS

3 pounds chicken pieces

1 pound onions, coarsely chopped

1 (28-ounce) can whole tomatoes, including juice

1 quart (4 cups) canned low-sodium chicken broth

Juice of 1 lemon

1 teaspoon crushed dried Italian seasoning

1 teaspoon sweet paprika

Garlic powder, to taste

2 bay leaves

Salt and freshly ground pepper, to taste

4 ounces very small whole wheat pasta, such as ditalini

Mexican Chicken Soup with Chipotle Chile

MAKES 4 SERVINGS

4 large bone-in chicken thighs
(about 1¾ pounds total)
1 dried or canned chipotle chile
1 medium onion, finely
chopped
2 cloves garlic, minced
1 medium red bell pepper,
finely chopped
1 teaspoon crushed dried
oregano
½ teaspoon crushed dried
thyme
½ teaspoon ground cumin
1 (14½-ounce) can diced
tomatoes, including juice
4 cups canned low-sodium
chicken broth
1 cup water
½ cup frozen corn kernels
4 scallions, white part and 1
inch green, chopped
¼ cup chopped fresh cilantro
¼ cup sour cream
4 lime wedges (optional)

Every country makes some variation of chicken soup—it's so warming and filling. In Mexico, it'll be laced with spices and herbs with added hotness from chiles. Such is the rendition of a soup I enjoyed at an outdoor restaurant in Puerto Vallarta.

A chipotle is actually a dried, smoked jalapeño chile. You'll find them dried or canned in adobo sauce in the Mexican aisle of a well-stocked supermarket or at a Mexican grocery store. If not available, add a teaspoon or so of chili powder. The sour cream and a squeeze of fresh lime just before eating will tone down the soup's heat.

Rinse the chicken; discard the skin and visible fat. Pat the chicken dry with paper towels and set aside. If using a dried chipotle, crush into a coarse powder. If using a canned chile, dice it. Place the chile, onion, garlic, bell pepper, oregano, thyme, and cumin in the bottom of a 3½-quart or larger crockery slow cooker. Arrange the chicken thighs on top.

In a bowl, combine the tomatoes with juice, broth, and water. Pour over the chicken. Cover and cook on LOW until the chicken is very tender when pierced with a fork, 7 to 7½ hours.

When the soup is almost done, add the corn kernels to enough boiling water to cover and boil for 2 minutes. Drain. Divide the corn among 4 wide, shallow soup bowls. Ladle the hot soup on top, making sure each serving gets 1 chicken thigh. Combine the scallions and cilantro. Place a dollop of sour cream in the center of each serving and sprinkle with the scallion–cilantro mixture. If using, offer the lime wedges to squeeze onto the soup before eating.

○ **PER SERVING:** 18 g carbohydrate (includes 3 g dietary fiber), 20 g protein, 10 g fat, 236 calories

○ **DIABETIC EXCHANGES:** ½ bread/starch, 2 vegetable, 2½ lean meat, ½ fat

Cock-a-Leekie

My mother used to make this Scottish soup, simmering it gently on the stove, and then years later, in one of the first Crock-Pots® manufactured. I didn't like the traditional addition of prunes in my soup, so she left them out. Now counting carbs, I still leave them out without diminishing the rich flavor of the soup. This is a warming whole-meal soup to have on a wintry night with some sharp cheddar cheese and crisp apples or pears.

MAKES 10 SERVINGS

3 pounds large leeks, trimmed with 3 inches green left on, well washed, and cut on the diagonal into 1-inch pieces

4 medium carrots, peeled and cut on the diagonal into 1-inch pieces

2 medium ribs celery, cut on the diagonal into 1-inch pieces

1/4 cup pearl barley, rinsed and drained

1 (3 1/2-pound) whole chicken, cut into quarters

2 (14-ounce) cans low-sodium chicken broth

2 cups water

6 whole black peppercorns

4 whole cloves

1/4 cup chopped fresh parsley

Place the leeks, carrots, celery, and barley in the bottom of a 5-quart or larger crockery slow cooker. Rinse the chicken; discard any visible fat. Pat the chicken dry with paper towels. Arrange on top of the leek mixture. Add the broth and water. Tie the peppercorns and cloves in a cheesecloth bag and add to the cooker.

Cover and cook on LOW for 7 to 9 hours or on HIGH for 3½ to 4½ hours. Transfer the chicken to a large plate and, when cool enough to handle, remove and discard the skin and bones. Cut the chicken into bite-size pieces and return to the cooker along with 2 tablespoons of the parsley. Ladle the soup into heated soup bowls and garnish each serving with some of the remaining parsley.

○ PER SERVING: 15 g carbohydrate (includes 2 g dietary fiber), 28 g protein, 7 g fat, 236 calories

○ DIABETIC EXCHANGES: 1/2 bread/starch, 2 vegetable, 3 1/2 very lean meat, 1 fat

Mulligatawny

MAKES 10 SERVINGS

2 medium onions, sliced

2 cloves garlic, minced

3 medium ribs celery with
leaves, chopped

2 carrots, peeled and chopped

3 medium plum tomatoes, cut
in half

½ cup dried yellow split peas

1 (2-inch) piece fresh ginger,
peeled and cut into ½-inch
pieces

1 (3½-pound) chicken,
quartered

1 tablespoon curry powder

1 teaspoon ground cumin

3 (14-ounce) cans low-sodium
chicken broth

1 cup water

4 parsley sprigs

1 bay leaf

½ cup nonfat plain yogurt for
garnish (optional)

2 medium plum tomatoes,
seeded and diced for garnish
(optional)

½ cup minced cilantro for
garnish (optional)

A great Indian restaurant just north of my former Connecticut home offers this marvelous curry soup on their luncheon menu. Not too spicy and rich with shreds of chicken, this is a wonderful soup to add to your slow-cooker repertoire.

Although the chef didn't give me an exact recipe, I was invited to visit him in the kitchen while he was making it and take notes. Then it was back to my own kitchen where I scaled down his recipe for 48 portions and came up with this close rendition. If your supermarket doesn't carry yellow split peas, look in a natural foods store or Indian market.

Place the onions, garlic, celery, carrots, halved tomatoes, split peas, and ginger in the bottom of a 5-quart or larger crockery slow cooker. Rinse the chicken; discard the skin and any fat. Arrange the chicken on top of the vegetables. Sprinkle with the curry powder and cumin. Pour the broth and water into the slow cooker and add the parsley and bay leaf.

Cover and cook on LOW for 7 to 10 hours or on HIGH for 3½ to 5 hours.

Transfer the chicken pieces to a large plate and, when cool enough to handle, discard the bones. Remove and discard the pieces of ginger, the parsley sprigs, and bay leaf. Shred the chicken and return to the cooker. Reheat the soup for a few minutes, and then ladle into heated soup bowls. If using, garnish each serving with a dollop of yogurt and a sprinkling of the tomatoes and cilantro. Serve hot.

○ PER SERVING: 13 g carbohydrate (includes 1 g dietary fiber), 31 g protein, 8 g fat, 248 calories

○ DIABETIC EXCHANGES: ½ bread/starch, 1 vegetable, 4 very lean meat, 1 fat

Hearty Chicken Soup with Wild Rice and Shiitake Mushrooms

Dubbed "rice" because it grows in water, wild rice is not rice at all. Instead, it is the seed of an annual marsh grass that grows in the glacier-carved wetlands of the northern Great Lakes. Wild rice is the only cereal grain native to North America, and even at 11½ grams of carbohydrate, including 1 gram of dietary fiber per ⅓ cup, cooked wild rice is sanctioned by low-carb diets. It adds a luxurious nutty flavor and chewy texture to this delicious, filling soup.

MAKES 8 SERVINGS

1 tablespoon canola oil

2 medium onions, sliced

2 medium ribs celery, chopped

1 clove garlic, minced

1 (3½-pound) chicken, cut into quarters

½ cup wild rice, rinsed and drained

½ teaspoon crushed dried thyme

2 cups dry white wine

4 cups canned low-sodium chicken broth

4 ounces shiitake or other wild mushrooms, trimmed, cleaned, and sliced

Salt and freshly ground pepper, to taste

¼ cup chopped fresh parsley

Heat the oil in a large nonstick skillet over medium heat. Add the onions, celery, and garlic. Sauté, stirring occasionally, until the vegetables are limp, about 4 minutes. Transfer the vegetables to the bottom of a 4-quart or larger crockery slow cooker.

Rinse the chicken; discard the skin and any visible fat. Pat dry with paper towels. Add the chicken pieces, 2 quarters at a time, to the skillet and brown on each side for 5 minutes, turning once. Transfer the browned chicken to the slow cooker. Repeat with the remaining quarters. Add the wild rice and thyme to the cooker. Pour in the wine and chicken broth.

Cover and cook on LOW for 5 to 6 hours or on HIGH for 2½ to 3 hours. Carefully remove the chicken pieces from the cooker and set aside to cool. When cool enough to handle, remove the chicken meat from the bones. Trim off any excess fat and dice the meat.

Return the chicken to the slow cooker along with the mushrooms. If cooking on LOW, increase the cooking temperature to HIGH. Cover and cook for another 10 to 15 minutes, until the mushrooms are tender. Taste and season with salt and pepper. Stir in the parsley and ladle the soup into heated shallow soup bowls. Serve immediately.

○ **PER SERVING:** 14 g carbohydrate (includes 1 g dietary fiber), 35 g protein, 10 g fat, 301 calories

○ **DIABETIC EXCHANGES:** ½ bread/starch, 1 vegetable, 4 very lean meat, 1½ fat

Asian Chicken Soup with Rice Stick Noodles

MAKES 8 SERVINGS

3 cups sliced shiitake
    mushroom caps
1 large onion, cut in half
    crosswise and then thinly
    sliced
1 tablespoon minced fresh
    ginger
2 cloves garlic, minced
1½ pounds boneless, skinless
    chicken breasts
2 (14-ounce) cans low-sodium
    chicken broth
2 tablespoons reduced-sodium
    soy sauce
6 ounces rice stick noodles
3 scallions, white part and 3
    inches green, julienned
1 small carrot, peeled and
    julienned
2 ounces snow peas, trimmed
    and julienned
Fresh cilantro leaves for
    garnish (optional)

It's easy to transform a pot of your mom's recipe for chicken soup into something exotic from another country by adding different vegetables, herbs, and spices. Here I've taken my mom's basic recipe and turned it into an Asian sensation.

Place the mushrooms, onion, ginger, and garlic in the bottom of a 3½-quart or larger crockery slow cooker. Rinse the chicken and discard all fat. Cut the chicken into 1-inch pieces. Add the chicken to the cooker. Combine the chicken broth and soy sauce; pour over the vegetables and chicken.

Cover and cook on LOW for 5 to 6 hours or on HIGH for 2½ to 3 hours. Near the end of the cooking time, prepare the rice stick noodles according to the package directions.

Meanwhile, add the scallions, carrot, and snow peas to the cooker. Re-cover and cook while the noodles are cooking. Drain the noodles and divide among 8 shallow heated soup bowls. Ladle the hot soup over the noodles. If using, sprinkle a few cilantro leaves on top and serve.

○ PER SERVING: 18 g carbohydrate (includes 2 g dietary fiber), 28 g protein, 4 g fat, 214 calories
○ DIABETIC EXCHANGES: ½ bread/starch, 2 vegetable, 3½ very lean meat

Beef and Barley Vegetable Soup

Lots of lean beef, barley, and vegetables simmer unattended all day to develop into this terrific-tasting soup.

Preheat the oven to 500°F. Arrange the beef cubes slightly apart in a single layer on a shallow baking pan. Bake until the beef is well browned, about 20 minutes.

Meanwhile, in a 3½-quart or larger crockery slow cooker, combine the onion, celery, carrots, parsnips, tomato, garlic, and barley. Transfer the browned beef to the cooker. Pour a little of the water into the baking pan and stir to dissolve the drippings. Add the mixture to the cooker along with the remaining water and beef broth.

Cover and cook on LOW about 8 hours or on HIGH about 4 hours, until the beef is very tender when pierced with a fork. Ladle into heated soup bowls and serve.

○ PER SERVING: 23 g carbohydrate (includes 5 g dietary fiber), 32 g protein, 25 g fat, 448 calories

○ DIABETIC EXCHANGES: ½ bread/starch, 3 vegetable, 4 lean meat, 2½ fat

MAKES 6 SERVINGS

2 pounds lean boneless beef chuck, trimmed of fat and cut into 1-inch cubes

1 large onion, thinly sliced

2 medium ribs celery with leaves, cut into 1-inch pieces

2 medium carrots, peeled and cut into 1-inch pieces

2 medium parsnips, peeled and cut into 1-inch pieces

1 medium tomato, seeded and coarsely chopped

3 cloves garlic, minced

¼ cup pearl barley, rinsed and drained

1½ cups water

2 (14-ounce) cans low-sodium beef broth

Sherried Beef Broth

MAKES 16 SERVINGS

8 cloves garlic, cut in half
1 tablespoon extra-virgin olive
    oil
8 cups homemade or canned
    low-sodium beef broth
2 cups dry sherry
Salt and freshly ground pepper,
    to taste
Thin lemon slices, for garnish

In my early professional days, I did a lot of catering for posh parties in the Los Angeles basin. This delightful soup was sipped at countless affairs—as a prelude to elegant meals at the Hollywood Bowl, stylish dinners in the garden, lavish buffets in front of the fireplace, and casual Super Bowl suppers in front of a giant-screen TV. Serve the soup in small mugs or teacups.

In a large nonstick skillet, sauté the garlic in the oil over medium heat until the garlic is soft but not browned. Transfer the garlic to a 3½-quart or larger crockery slow cooker. Stir in the broth and sherry.

Cover and cook on HIGH for 1 hour. Discard the garlic cloves. Taste the soup and season as needed with salt and pepper. Ladle the broth into heated mugs or teacups and float a lemon slice on top.

○ PER SERVING: 1 g carbohydrate (includes trace dietary fiber), 3 g protein, 2 g fat, 34 calories
○ DIABETIC EXCHANGES: ½ lean meat

Chipotle Steak and Shiitake Mushroom Soup

When you're hungry for steak but don't want the heavy meal that usually accompanies it, this wonderful soup may be the satisfying dinner solution. I can buy jars of whole roasted red bell peppers in the produce section of my supermarket. Look for chipotle chiles in the Mexican food aisle.

MAKES 6 SERVINGS

4 slices bacon, cut into ½-inch pieces

2 pounds lean boneless beef sirloin, trimmed of all fat and cut into 1-inch cubes

2 medium onions, chopped

2 cloves garlic, minced

3 canned chipotle chiles in adobo sauce, chopped

1 pound fresh shiitake mushrooms, cleaned, stems discarded, and caps sliced

6 cups canned low-sodium beef broth

3 large roasted red bell peppers, drained and cut into thin julienne strips

In a large nonstick skillet over medium heat, sauté the bacon until lightly browned. Using a slotted spoon, transfer the bacon to a 4-quart or larger crockery slow cooker. Discard the drippings and add the beef to the same skillet. Sauté over medium heat, stirring frequently, until the beef is browned on all sides, about 5 minutes. Add the beef to the slow cooker along with the onions, garlic, chiles, and mushrooms. Stir in the beef broth.

Cover and cook on LOW for 8 to 10 hours or on HIGH for 4 to 5 hours. Divide the roasted pepper strips among 6 wide, shallow, heated soup bowls. Ladle the hot soup over the peppers and serve.

○ **PER SERVING:** 18 g carbohydrate (includes 3 g dietary fiber), 38 g protein, 18 g fat, 391 calories

○ **DIABETIC EXCHANGES:** 3 vegetable, 5 lean meat, 1 fat

Harira (Lamb and Chickpea Soup)

MAKES 6 SERVINGS

2 medium onions, chopped

2 medium ribs celery with
  leaves, diced

2 cloves garlic, minced

2 teaspoons sweet paprika

1 teaspoon ground cumin

½ teaspoon ground ginger

¼ teaspoon freshly ground
  pepper

¼ teaspoon crushed saffron
  threads

1 pound lean lamb stew meat,
  trimmed of fat

1 (14½-ounce) can chopped
  tomatoes, including juices

2 (14-ounce) cans low-sodium
  beef broth

1 cup water

3 tablespoons fresh lemon juice

1 (15-ounce) can chickpeas
  (garbanzo beans), rinsed and
  drained

1 (3-inch) cinnamon stick

½ cup chopped fresh cilantro

One of the reasons that I love traveling by cruise ship is that it gives me a "taste" of a lot of cultures and different cuisines in a short time, especially on the smaller ships, which my husband and I prefer. Such was the case on our most recent Mediterranean cruise when we sailed through the Straits of Gibraltar where the lights of Morocco were on the starboard side of the dining room and the lights of Spain were on the port side. The evening's dinner menu was a mix of the two cuisines, and, for a starter, Harira was offered. I'd never tasted this lamb soup before so I gave it a try. It was so delicious that I later interviewed the chef to ascertain the soup's basic ingredients and principles. After experimenting in my kitchen back home, I came up with this version, which I make frequently.

If you can spare the extra carbs, serve this soup with toasted wedges of whole wheat pita bread drizzled with some extra-virgin olive oil for a complete, satisfying meal.

HOW TO ROAST BELL PEPPERS

Preheat the broiler. Place the bell peppers in a shallow baking pan and broil about 3 inches from the source of heat until the skins are charred, turning occasionally. This should take 12 to 15 minutes.

Remove the peppers from the oven and place in a plastic or paper bag. Close the bag tightly and let steam for 15 minutes. Remove and let the peppers cool until you can handle them. Slip off the skins, cut in half lengthwise, and remove the core and seeds. Use as directed in desired recipe or place in a covered container and refrigerate for up to 3 days, or freeze for up to 1 month.

Place the onions, celery, and garlic in the bottom of a 3½-quart or larger crockery slow cooker. Add the lamb to the cooker. Combine the paprika, cumin, ginger, pepper, and saffron, and rub into all sides of the lamb. Stir in the tomatoes and their juices, beef broth, water, and lemon juice. Add the chickpeas and submerge the cinnamon stick.

Cover and cook on LOW until the lamb is very tender when pierced with a fork, 7 to 8 hours. If using the HIGH setting, cook for 3½ to 4 hours. When the soup is done, discard the cinnamon stick and stir in the cilantro. Ladle into soup bowls and serve immediately.

○ PER SERVING: 29 g carbohydrate (includes 7 g dietary fiber), 32 g protein, 9 g fat, 318 calories
○ DIABETIC EXCHANGES: 1 bread/starch, 1½ vegetable, 4 very lean meat, 1 fat

Peasant Soup

MAKES 8 SERVINGS

1 large onion, chopped

3 medium leeks, white part only, well washed and thinly sliced

4 cloves garlic, minced

1 ham hock

3 ribs celery with some leaves, chopped

2 medium carrots, peeled and chopped

2 medium parsnips, peeled and chopped

1 medium turnip, peeled and chopped

6 cups canned low-sodium chicken broth

1 teaspoon crushed dried Italian herb seasoning

1 bay leaf

1 (15-ounce) can Great Northern or navy beans, rinsed and drained

½ cup shredded fontina cheese

This old-fashioned soup, made with a ham hock and hearty vegetables, will generate warmth on the bleakest of fall or winter days. Sprinkle the steaming bowls of this soup with shredded fontina cheese.

Place the onion, leeks, and garlic in the bottom of a 4-quart or larger crockery slow cooker. Add the ham hock and surround with the celery, carrots, parsnips, and turnip. Pour in the broth and sprinkle with the Italian seasoning. Submerge the bay leaf.

Cover and cook on LOW for 10 to 11 hours or on HIGH for 4½ to 5 hours. Remove the ham hock and allow to cool slightly. Discard the bay leaf. Cut the meat off the bone; dice the meat and return it to the slow cooker along with the beans. If cooking on LOW, increase the temperature setting to HIGH. Cover and cook for another 15 minutes.

Ladle into heated soup bowls. Sprinkle each serving with 1 tablespoon cheese. Serve immediately.

○ PER SERVING: 26 g carbohydrate (includes 6 g dietary fiber), 10 g protein, 5 g fat, 188 calories

○ DIABETIC EXCHANGES: ½ bread/starch, 3 vegetable, 1 lean meat, ½ fat

Farmhouse Vegetable Soup

When the frigid winds start to blow south from Canada, nothing's more comforting than the aroma of soup simmering away when you walk into the kitchen. Whether you serve this soup as a first course or the main meal, it's sure to be soul-satisfying.

Pick over the lentils, discarding any stones or damaged lentils. Rinse and drain. Place in a 3½-quart or larger crockery slow cooker along with the leeks, garlic, fennel, carrots, turnip, thyme, and bay leaf. Stir in the tomatoes with juices and the broth.

Cover and cook on LOW for 9½ to 11½ hours or on HIGH for 4½ to 5½ hours.

Uncover and stir in the cabbage. If cooking on LOW, raise the temperature setting to HIGH. Re-cover and cook until the cabbage is just tender, about 30 minutes. Discard the bay leaf.

Ladle into heated soup bowls. If using, sprinkle with parsley. Serve hot.

○ **PER SERVING:** 25 g carbohydrate (includes 6 g dietary fiber), 8 g protein, 2 g fat, 139 calories

○ **DIABETIC EXCHANGES:** ½ bread/starch, 3 vegetable, ½ lean meat

MAKES 6 SERVINGS

⅓ cup dried brown lentils

3 medium leeks, trimmed, washed, and thinly sliced

3 cloves garlic, minced

1 medium bulb fennel, trimmed and thinly sliced

2 medium carrots, peeled and diced

1 medium white turnip, peeled and diced

1 teaspoon crushed dried thyme

1 bay leaf

1 (14½-ounce) can Italian plum tomatoes, including juice

6 cups canned low-sodium chicken broth or vegetable broth

2 cups shredded green cabbage

Minced parsley, for garnish (optional)

Curried Cream of Cauliflower and Apple Soup

MAKES 8 SERVINGS

1 tablespoon unsalted butter

1 cup chopped onion

4 cups canned low-sodium chicken broth

1 tablespoon curry powder

¼ teaspoon saffron threads

2 medium Granny Smith apples, cored, peeled, and chopped

1½ pounds cauliflower florets, trimmed

1 cup evaporated skim milk

Salt and freshly ground pepper, to taste

12 fresh chives, for garnish (optional)

⅓ cup minced red bell pepper, for garnish (optional)

This is my favorite soup to serve before any festive winter meal, especially Christmas Eve supper when I garnish it with chives and bits of minced red bell pepper. It simmers away during the day without attention and will keep hot until you're ready to serve.

Melt the butter in a nonstick skillet over medium heat. Add the onion and sauté until the onion is limp but not browned, about 4 minutes. In a 3½-quart crockery slow cooker, combine the onion with the broth, curry powder, saffron, apples, and cauliflower.

Cover and cook on LOW for 6 to 7 hours or on HIGH for 3 to 3½ hours, until the cauliflower is very tender. Transfer in batches to a food processor and purée until very smooth. Return to the cooker and stir in the evaporated milk. Taste and season with salt and pepper. Cover and keep on LOW until heated through, about 30 minutes.

To serve, ladle into heated soup bowls. If using, float 2 chives on each serving, crossing at the top. Sprinkle the bell pepper in between. Serve immediately.

○ **PER SERVING:** 15 g carbohydrate (includes 4 g dietary fiber), 6 g protein, 3 g fat, 102 calories

○ **DIABETIC EXCHANGES:** ½ skim milk, 1 vegetable

Crockery French Onion Soup

You can simmer this soup in your slow cooker for as long as all day or as little as 2½ hours. Because we're all counting carbs, the customary French bread and Swiss Gruyère cheese crouton has been forfeited for slivers of Brie cheese. The result is delicious!

Heat the butter and olive oil in a large nonstick skillet over medium-high heat. Add the onions and sauté, stirring frequently, until softened, about 5 minutes. Reduce the heat to low, cover, and cook until the onions are tender, about 15 minutes, stirring occasionally.

Uncover the skillet and sprinkle with the sugar. Raise the heat to medium-high and cook, stirring frequently, until the onions are golden and begin to caramelize, about 10 minutes.

Transfer the onions to a 3½-quart or larger crockery slow cooker. Stir in the broth, vermouth, and Worcestershire sauce. Cover and cook on LOW for 5 to 10 hours or on HIGH for 2½ to 3 hours. Taste and season with salt and pepper.

When ready to serve, distribute the scallions and cheese slivers among 8 heated soup bowls. Ladle the hot soup on top and serve.

○ PER SERVING: 17 g carbohydrate (includes 2 g dietary fiber), 7 g protein, 8 g fat, 161 calories
○ DIABETIC EXCHANGES: 3 vegetable, ½ lean meat, 1 fat

MAKES 10 SERVINGS

2 tablespoons unsalted butter
1 tablespoon olive oil
3 pounds (4 to 5 large) yellow or white onions, thinly sliced
2 teaspoons sugar
5 cups canned low-sodium beef broth
½ cup dry vermouth or additional broth
1 teaspoon Worcestershire sauce
Salt and freshly ground pepper, to taste
1 bunch scallions, trimmed and minced, including some green
4 ounces Brie cheese, cut into thin slivers

Spanish Onion and Almond Soup

MAKES 6 SERVINGS

3 large onions, thinly sliced

5 cups canned low-sodium
   chicken broth

1 cup dry white wine or
   additional broth

$^1/_8$ teaspoon ground cumin

2 sprigs parsley

$^1/_3$ cup slivered blanched
   almonds

$^1/_2$ cup shredded Swiss cheese

$^1/_4$ cup sliced almonds, toasted

While this soup contains some of the same ingredients as the French version, it's deliciously different. I first encountered this soup in a café in Barcelona; it was offered years later on the dinner menu of our cruise ship after a day in Malaga and Granada. In my version, I'm foregoing the bread crouton, but not skimping on the cheese and almond garnish.

In a 4-quart or larger crockery slow cooker, combine the onions, broth, wine, and cumin. Add the parsley, cover, and cook on LOW for 8 to 10 hours or on HIGH for 4 to 5 hours. Discard the parsley.

In the work bowl of a food processor, pulse the slivered almonds until finely chopped. Add ½ cup of the soup broth and process until smooth and the mixture appears milky. Return the broth with the almonds to the soup. If cooking on LOW, raise the temperature setting to HIGH. Cover and cook for another 30 minutes.

To serve, distribute the Swiss cheese among 6 heated soup bowls. Ladle the hot soup over the cheese and sprinkle with the toasted almonds. Serve at once.

○ PER SERVING: 10 g carbohydrate (includes 2 g dietary fiber), 8 g protein, 10 g fat, 159 calories

○ DIABETIC EXCHANGES: 1 vegetable, 1 lean meat, 1½ fat

Caramelized Garlic Soup

This is a terrific soup to chase away the winter chill. Roasted heads of garlic are combined with chicken broth and chipotle chiles for a savory version of the garlic-bread soup of southern France. Baked strips of low-carb tortillas take the place of the traditional toasted peasant bread.

Squeeze the roasted garlic cloves into the bottom of a 3½-quart or larger crockery slow cooker. Discard the skins. Add the onion, chicken broth, lime juice, chipotle chiles, oregano, cumin, and coriander.

Cover and cook on LOW for 7 to 9 hours or on HIGH for 3½ to 4½ hours. Meanwhile, preheat the oven to 450°F. Lightly oil a baking sheet. Arrange the tortilla strips in a single layer on the baking sheet and bake for 5 to 7 minutes, tossing the strips occasionally, until crisp. Set aside.

When ready to serve, place 1 tablespoon of the cheese in a pile in each of 8 shallow soup bowls. Lay an avocado slice on top of each cheese pile. Ladle the hot soup into the bowls and top each serving with a scattering of tortilla strips and some of the cilantro. Serve immediately.

○ PER SERVING: 12 g carbohydrate (includes 5 g dietary fiber), 7 g protein, 7 g fat, 129 calories
○ DIABETIC EXCHANGES: ½ vegetable, ½ lean meat, 1 fat

MAKES 8 SERVINGS

2 heads garlic, roasted (see page 165)

1 medium red onion, cut in quarters and thinly sliced

6 cups canned low-sodium chicken broth

¼ cup fresh lime juice

3 canned chipotle chiles in adobo sauce, drained and chopped

½ teaspoon crushed dried oregano

½ teaspoon ground cumin

¼ teaspoon ground coriander

Canola oil

4 (6½-inch) low-carb whole-wheat tortillas, cut into thin strips

½ cup shredded Monterey Jack cheese

1 large Hass avocado, peeled, seeded, and sliced lengthwise into eighths

¼ cup chopped fresh cilantro

Slow-Cooked Minestrone

MAKES 8 SERVINGS

1 medium onion, finely diced

1 shallot, finely diced

1 clove garlic, minced

2 medium carrots, peeled and
diced

1 medium rib celery, diced

1 small Japanese eggplant,
peeled and diced

1 (14½-ounce) can Italian plum
tomatoes, including juices

5 cups canned low-sodium
chicken broth or vegetable
broth

1 teaspoon crushed dried
oregano

½ teaspoon crushed dried basil

½ teaspoon crushed dried
thyme

⅛ teaspoon crushed dried
rosemary

8 ounces fresh kale, trimmed
and shredded

1 cup canned cranberry beans,
drained and rinsed

Salt and freshly ground pepper,
to taste

1 ounce Parmesan or Romano
cheese, thinly shaved

Another great vegetable soup, this one is redolent with Italian flavors. It's even better the next day, so don't worry if you have leftovers. Cranberry beans are superb in this soup, but if not available, you can substitute canned cannellini.

In a 3½-quart or larger crockery slow cooker, combine the onion, shallot, garlic, carrots, celery, eggplant, and tomatoes with juices. Stir in the chicken broth, oregano, basil, thyme, and rosemary.

Cover and cook on LOW for 7½ to 9½ hours or on HIGH for 3½ to 4½ hours. Uncover and add the kale and cranberry beans. If cooking on LOW, raise the temperature setting to HIGH. Re-cover and cook on HIGH for another 30 minutes, until the kale is cooked and the beans are heated through. Taste and season with salt and pepper.

Ladle into heated, wide, shallow soup bowls. Sprinkle with Parmesan cheese and serve at once.

○ PER SERVING: 20 g carbohydrate (includes 6 g dietary fiber), 9 g protein, 3 g fat, 136 calories

○ DIABETIC EXCHANGES: ½ bread/starch, 2 vegetable, ½ lean meat

Savory Cream of Tomato Soup

When my mom made tomato soup, she always added a bit of baking soda to tame the acids of the tomatoes. Don't be alarmed at the amount of garlic in this soup—it mellows and sweetens with the slow cooking.

Place the tomatoes in the bottom of a 3½-quart or larger crockery slow cooker. Sprinkle with the garlic and onion. Season with salt and pepper. Top with the brown sugar, thyme, and basil. Drizzle with the olive oil and balsamic vinegar.

Cover and cook on LOW for 6 to 8 hours, until the vegetables are tender. Add the tomato sauce, tomato juice, and baking soda. Stir well. Stir in the evaporated milk. Cover and cook another 30 to 40 minutes, until the flavors blend and the soup is heated through. Ladle the hot soup into heated soup bowls and serve.

○ PER SERVING: 18 g carbohydrate (includes 2 g dietary fiber), 5 g protein, 2 g fat, 107 calories
○ DIABETIC EXCHANGES: ½ skim milk, 1½ vegetable, ½ fat

MAKES 8 SERVINGS

1½ pounds plum tomatoes, seeded and diced

12 cloves garlic, minced

1 medium red onion, diced

Salt and freshly ground pepper, to taste

2 teaspoons light brown sugar

2 teaspoons crushed dried thyme

1 teaspoon crushed dried basil

1 tablespoon extra-virgin olive oil

2 tablespoons balsamic vinegar

1 (8-ounce) can tomato sauce

½ cup tomato juice

½ teaspoon baking soda

1 (12-ounce) can evaporated skim milk

Newport Clam Chowder

MAKES 6 SERVINGS

3 slices bacon, cooked crisp, drained, and crumbled

3 ounces new potatoes, scrubbed and diced into ½-inch cubes

1 medium onion, chopped

3 medium ribs celery with leaves, chopped

1 small red bell pepper, seeded and chopped

1 pint minced fresh clams or 2 (6½-ounce) cans minced clams

1 (14½-ounce) can diced tomatoes, including juices

1½ cups bottled clam juice or canned low-sodium chicken broth

½ teaspoon crushed dried thyme

¼ teaspoon freshly ground pepper

½ teaspoon crushed red pepper flakes

2 bay leaves

2 tablespoons minced fresh parsley, for garnish (optional)

2 tablespoons minced fresh chives, for garnish (optional)

1½ cups milk, heated until hot

At the chowder house that used to be on the pier in Newport, Rhode Island, they served chowder like this with a pitcher of hot milk to pour into the soup. Serve this robust chowder as a prelude to a light meal or as a meal by itself.

Place the bacon, potatoes, onion, celery, and bell pepper in the bottom of a 3½-quart or larger crockery slow cooker. Drain the clams and add their juice to the cooker. Place the clams in a small dish, cover, and refrigerate. Add the tomatoes with juices and the bottled clam juice to the cooker. Stir in the thyme, pepper, and red pepper flakes. Add the bay leaves.

Cover and cook on LOW for 8 to 10 hours or on HIGH for 4 to 5 hours.

If cooking on LOW, increase the cooker setting to HIGH and stir in the reserved clams. Cover and cook for 10 minutes more. Remove the bay leaves. Ladle the chowder into bowls and, if using, sprinkle each serving with some of the parsley and chives. Place the hot milk in a pitcher and pass to pour over each serving.

○ **PER SERVING:** 14 g carbohydrate (includes 1 g dietary fiber), 9 g protein, 4 g fat, 124 calories

○ **DIABETIC EXCHANGES:** 1½ vegetable, 1 very lean meat, ½ fat

Hearty Mediterranean Fish Soup

For easy weekday meals, put this soup on to cook first thing in the morning so you can be away all day. All you need to complete the meal is a big green salad and an array of fresh fruit and cheese for dessert. Even your most discerning guest will think you've been slaving away in the kitchen all day. I can buy top-quality frozen fish stock at my market; if it's not available in yours, use bottled clam juice.

Throughout much of Provence, this soup is puréed before serving, but when I had it at the Hotel Byblos in St. Tropez, it was served in this manner.

In a large nonstick skillet, heat the oil over medium heat. Add the leeks, fennel, carrot, shallots, and garlic. Sauté, stirring occasionally, until the vegetables are wilted, about 10 minutes. Transfer to a 3½-quart or larger crockery slow cooker. Stir in the tomatoes with juices, the stock, wine, thyme, saffron, bay leaf, 2 teaspoons orange zest, and cayenne.

Cover and cook on LOW for 4 to 5 hours or on HIGH for 2 to 2½ hours. If cooking on LOW, increase the cooking temperature to HIGH. Taste and add salt and pepper as needed. Rinse the fish and pat dry. Cut the fish crosswise on the diagonal into strips about 1 inch wide. Add the fish to the cooker, cover, and cook until the fish is just cooked through, about 15 minutes.

Ladle the soup into heated shallow soup bowls and, if using, garnish with parsley and some of the additional orange zest. Serve immediately.

○ PER SERVING: 14 g carbohydrate (3 g dietary fiber), 32 g protein, 6 g fat, 239 calories

○ DIABETIC EXCHANGES: 2½ vegetable, 4½ very lean meat, ½ fat

MAKES 6 SERVINGS

1 tablespoon extra-virgin olive oil

3 medium leeks, white and pale green parts, sliced in half lengthwise, well washed, and thinly sliced

1 medium fennel bulb, trimmed and chopped

1 medium carrot, peeled and diced

2 shallots, minced

2 cloves garlic, minced

1 (14½-ounce) can Italian plum tomatoes, including juices

4 cups fish stock or bottled clam juice

1 cup dry white wine or additional stock

½ teaspoon crushed dried thyme

¼ teaspoon saffron threads, crumbled

1 bay leaf

2 teaspoons grated orange zest plus 1 tablespoon additional, for garnish (optional)

⅛ teaspoon cayenne pepper

Salt and freshly ground pepper, to taste

2 pounds white-fleshed fish fillets (such as snapper, grouper, or sea bass), skinned

Chopped parsley, for garnish (optional)

Dixie-Style Chicken Stew

MAKES 4 SERVINGS

1¼ pounds boneless, skinless chicken thighs

2 teaspoons extra-virgin olive oil

1 medium onion, chopped

2 cloves garlic, minced

1 medium rib celery, chopped

1 teaspoon Creole or Cajun seasoning

1 (10-ounce) package frozen cut okra

6 dry-pack sun-dried tomatoes, chopped

1 (14½-ounce) can stewed tomatoes, including juice

1 (14½-ounce) can low-sodium chicken broth

1 (10-ounce) package frozen black-eyed peas, thawed

4 cups chopped fresh collard greens or spinach

This hearty stew features familiar Southern ingredients—chicken, tomatoes, black-eyed peas, okra, and collard greens. The addition of dry-pack sun-dried tomatoes intensifies the tomato flavor. Don't forget to set a bottle of Tabasco or your favorite hot sauce on the table to sprinkle onto each serving.

Rinse the chicken thighs; discard any visible fat. Pat dry and cut into 1-inch pieces. Heat the oil in a large nonstick skillet over medium-high heat. Add the chicken and sauté for 5 to 6 minutes, stirring often to brown all sides.

Transfer the chicken to a 3½-quart or larger crockery slow cooker. Stir in the onion, garlic, celery, Creole seasoning, okra, sun-dried tomatoes, tomatoes with juices, and the broth.

Cover and cook on LOW for 6 to 8 hours or on HIGH for 3½ to 4½ hours. If cooking on LOW, increase the temperature setting to HIGH. Stir in the black-eyed peas and collard greens. Cover and cook about 10 minutes more. Ladle into bowls to serve.

○ PER SERVING: 36 g carbohydrate (9 g dietary fiber), 39 g protein, 9 g fat, 380 calories

○ DIABETIC EXCHANGES: 1 bread/starch, 3½ vegetable, 4 very lean meat, 1 fat

Chicken and Spicy Sausage Stew

You can change this delicious stew from Italian to Cajun or Mexican by the type of sausage, stewed tomatoes, and herbs that you use.

Place the onion and sweet potato pieces in the bottom of a 3½-quart or larger crockery slow cooker. Rinse the chicken and remove any fat. Pat the chicken dry with paper towels. Cut the chicken into 1-inch cubes. Heat the olive oil in a large nonstick skillet over medium-high heat. Add the chicken pieces and sauté for 3 to 4 minutes, stirring constantly. Using a slotted spoon, transfer the chicken to the slow cooker.

Remove the casings from the sausage and cut the sausage into small chunks. Add the sausage to the skillet and sauté for 5 minutes, stirring occasionally. Using a slotted spoon, transfer the sausage pieces to the slow cooker. Sprinkle with the tomatoes with juices and the Italian seasoning; pour the broth over the mixture.

Cover and cook on LOW for 6 to 7 hours or on HIGH for 3 to 3½ hours. If cooking on LOW, increase the cooking temperature to HIGH. Add the lima beans, cover, and cook for 15 to 20 minutes, until the lima beans are just tender. Ladle into heated bowls and serve.

○ PER SERVING: 29 g carbohydrate (includes 7 g dietary fiber), 32 g protein, 13 g fat, 357 calories

○ DIABETIC EXCHANGES: 1 bread/starch, 1½ vegetable, 1 very lean meat, 3 lean meat, 1½ fat

MAKES 4 SERVINGS

1 medium onion, thinly sliced

1 (10-ounce) sweet potato, peeled and cut into 12 pieces

2 (6-ounce) boneless, skinless chicken breast halves

1 tablespoon extra-virgin olive oil

8 ounces hot Italian sausage, andouille sausage, or Mexican chorizo

1 (14½-ounce) can Italian-, Cajun-, or Mexican-style stewed tomatoes, including juice

1 teaspoon crushed Italian seasoning, Cajun seasoning, or Mexican seasoning

1 (14-ounce) can low-sodium chicken broth

1 cup frozen lima beans

Savory Chicken Stew, Italian Style

MAKES 4 SERVINGS

1 medium onion, chopped

2 cloves garlic, minced

1 pound boneless, skinless chicken breasts

1 (6-ounce) package sliced mushrooms

1 (14½-ounce) can Italian stewed tomatoes, including juices

1 small red bell pepper, cut into thin julienne strips

2 tablespoons tomato paste

2 tablespoons dry red wine

2 teaspoons crushed Italian herb seasoning (see headnote)

2 bay leaves

Here's an easy stew with lots of Italian flavor. You'll find jars of Italian herb seasoning in the spice aisle of your supermarket, or for the 2 teaspoons of seasoning, you can use ½ teaspoon each of crushed dried basil, dried marjoram, dried oregano, and thyme.

Place the onion and garlic in the bottom of a 3½-quart or larger crockery slow cooker. Rinse the chicken; discard any fat. Cut the chicken into 1-inch pieces. Add the chicken, mushrooms, tomatoes with juices, and bell pepper to the cooker. Combine the tomato paste and red wine. Add to the cooker. Stir in the Italian seasoning and submerge the bay leaves in the liquid.

Cover and cook on LOW for 5 to 6 hours or on HIGH for 2½ to 3 hours, until the chicken is cooked through. Discard the bay leaves and ladle into shallow soup bowls. Serve hot.

○ PER SERVING: 14 g carbohydrate (includes 3 g dietary fiber), 27 g protein, 11 g fat, 261 calories

○ DIABETIC EXCHANGES: 2 vegetable, 3½ lean meat

Moroccan Chicken Stew

When we were cruising off the coast of Morocco, the ship's dining room offered a chicken tagine (stew) similar to this—flavored with cinnamon, orange zest, dates, and tomatoes. Because dates are very high in carbs, I've allowed only 1 date per serving with little loss of the stew's integrity. This is traditionally served over a bowl of couscous, which I've made optional.

MAKES 6 SERVINGS

1 medium Sweet Dumpling or acorn squash
1 medium onion, thinly sliced
3 cloves garlic, minced
6 (5-ounce) boneless, skinless chicken thighs
Salt and freshly ground pepper, to taste
$\frac{1}{2}$ teaspoon ground cinnamon
$\frac{1}{2}$ teaspoon ground ginger
$\frac{1}{4}$ teaspoon crumbled saffron threads
1 tablespoon grated orange zest
2 cups canned low-sodium chicken broth
1 cup canned chickpeas (garbanzo beans), drained and rinsed
6 large pitted dates, halved
3 ripe plum tomatoes, seeded and cut into $\frac{1}{2}$-inch dice
$\frac{1}{2}$ cup chopped fresh parsley
$\frac{1}{4}$ cup chopped fresh mint
2 cups cooked couscous (optional)

Cut the squash into ¾-inch-thick rings and remove the seeds. Cut the rings into quarters and remove the skin with a vegetable peeler. Arrange the squash in the bottom of a 3½-quart or larger crockery slow cooker. Top with the onion and garlic.

Rinse the chicken thighs; remove all fat. Pat the chicken dry with paper towels. Cut into thin, crosswise strips. Season the chicken with salt and pepper. In a small bowl, combine the cinnamon, ginger, and saffron. Sprinkle half of the mixture over the vegetables and half over the chicken. Add the chicken to the slow cooker and sprinkle with the orange zest. Pour the broth over all.

Cover and cook on LOW for 5 to 6 hours or on HIGH for 2½ to 3 hours, until the chicken is cooked through. During the last 30 minutes of cooking (15 minutes if cooking on HIGH), add the chickpeas, dates, and tomatoes. Just before serving, stir in the parsley and mint. If using, place ⅓ cup of the couscous in the middle of 6 shallow bowls. Distribute the chicken, vegetables, and dates evenly amond the bowls and serve immediately.

○ **PER SERVING (STEW ONLY):** 33 g carbohydrate (includes 5 g dietary fiber), 22 g protein, 7 g fat, 280 calories
○ **DIABETIC EXCHANGES:** $\frac{1}{2}$ bread/starch, 1 fruit, 1 vegetable, 2$\frac{1}{2}$ very lean meat

Chicken Bouillabaisse with Rouille

MAKES 6 SERVINGS

2 pounds skinless chicken
  breast halves and thighs
Salt and freshly ground pepper,
  to taste
1 tablespoon extra-virgin olive
  oil
2 large leeks, white part and 1
  inch pale green, well
  washed and minced
3 ounces very small red new
  potatoes, scrubbed and cut
  into ¹⁄₂-inch rounds
1 medium onion, minced
3 cloves garlic, minced
3 medium, ripe tomatoes,
  seeded and minced
2 teaspoons grated orange zest
1 teaspoon crushed dried thyme
¹⁄₄ teaspoon crushed red pepper
  flakes
2 cups canned low-sodium
  chicken broth
1 cup dry white wine or
  additional broth
¹⁄₂ teaspoon crumbled saffron
  threads
Rouille (see page 49); (optional)

You don't have to use seafood when you make bouillabaisse, the cele-brated stew of Provence. Made with chicken, it's equally delicious. If the rouille—the fiery sauce traditionally served with the stew—brings your carb count too high, forego it in favor of a sprinkling of crushed red pepper flakes and a light drizzle of extra-virgin olive oil.

Rinse the chicken pieces; remove any visible fat. Pat the chicken dry with paper towels and season with salt and pepper. Heat the olive oil in a large nonstick skillet over medium-high heat. Add the chicken, a few pieces at a time, and brown, turning once, about 10 minutes. Transfer the browned chicken to the bottom of a 3½-quart or larger crockery slow cooker. Repeat until all the chicken is browned. Add the leeks, potatoes, onion, garlic, and tomatoes to the slow cooker. Sprinkle with the orange zest, thyme, and red pepper flakes. Pour in the broth and wine.

Cover and cook on LOW for 6 to 7 hours or on HIGH for 3 to 3½ hours, until the chicken is cooked through and the veg-etables are tender. Transfer the chicken and vegetables to a large, heated serving bowl. Skim off any fat on the cooking liquid and, if cooking on LOW, increase the temperature setting to HIGH. Stir in the saffron and cook, uncovered, until thickened slightly, 5 to 10 minutes. Pour the pan sauce over the chicken and serve immediately. Pass the rouille separately to spoon onto each serv-ing, if using.

○ PER SERVING (BOUILLABAISSE ONLY): 10 g carbohydrate (includes 2 g
  dietary fiber), 32 g protein, 10 g fat, 266 calories
○ DIABETIC EXCHANGES: 1¹⁄₂ vegetable, 4¹⁄₂ protein, 1¹⁄₂ fat

Rouille

Tear the bread into small pieces and moisten with the wine. Place in the work bowl of a food processor. In a small dish, moisten the saffron with the hot water. Scrape the mixture into the food processor and add the garlic, salt, and red pepper flakes. Process to a smooth paste. With the motor running, pour the olive oil through the feed tube. Process to a creamy purée. Transfer the rouille to a small serving dish and pass to spoon into the hot bouillabaisse.

○ PER 1-TABLESPOON SERVING (ROUILLE ONLY): 2 g carbohydrate (includes trace dietary fiber), 1 g protein, 4 g fat, 44 calories
○ DIABETIC EXCHANGES: 1 fat

MAKES ABOUT ½ CUP

1 slice whole wheat bread
2 tablespoons dry white wine
¼ teaspoon crumbled saffron threads
½ tablespoon hot water
2 cloves garlic, cut in half
½ teaspoon salt
¼ to ½ teaspoon crushed red pepper flakes
2 tablespoons extra-virgin olive oil

SAFFRON

Saffron—the dried, deep orange–red stigmas from a small purple crocus—is the world's most expensive spice. The reason for the expense is that it must be hand-picked and, with only 3 stigmas per flower, it takes almost 70,000 flowers to produce 1 pound of saffron. That's almost 12 days of hard work for an experienced picker. Fortunately, a little saffron goes a long way. It's integral to hundreds of dishes, especially those of the Mediterranean and Europe. You can achieve a similar yellow color, although a different taste, by using the less expensive spice turmeric.

Provençal Beef Stew

MAKES 6 SERVINGS

2 pounds lean boneless beef
    sirloin, cut 1 inch thick
1 tablespoon *herbes de Provence*
    (see page 67)
5 shallots, thinly sliced
5 cloves garlic, thinly sliced
⅓ cup finely chopped lean ham
1 tablespoon minced orange
    zest
2 tablespoons balsamic or red
    wine vinegar
¾ cup dry red wine or low-
    sodium canned beef broth
¼ cup brandy, additional wine,
    or beef broth
4 anchovy fillets, drained
    (optional)
2 tablespoons all-purpose flour
2 tablespoons unsalted butter,
    softened
1 tablespoon capers, rinsed and
    drained
Chopped parsley, for garnish
    (optional)

A hearty stew is called a daube *in Provence and is usually a guarded family recipe cooked in a sealed earthenware casserole. This kind of slow cooking is tailor-made for a crockery slow cooker. Years ago, a California neighbor's grandmother who lived in St. Rémy, the village made famous by the paintings of van Gogh, sent me this recipe. She marinated the beef overnight in olive oil and garlic, but I find that unnecessary when cooking in a slow cooker. Eliminating that step also lowers the fat considerably.*

The herbes de Provence—*shallots, garlic, anchovies, and capers—are all flavors of this region in southern France.*

Trim fat from the beef and cut into 6 equal pieces. Season both sides with the *herbes de Provence*. In a bowl, combine the shallots, garlic, ham, and orange zest. Place one-third of the mixture in the bottom of a 3½-quart or larger crockery slow cooker. Place 3 pieces of the beef on top, and then sprinkle with one-third of the shallot–ham mixture. Repeat the layering once more with the last of the beef and the shallot–ham mixture. Drizzle with the vinegar and pour in the wine and brandy.

Cover and cook on LOW for 8 to 9 hours or on HIGH for 3½ to 4½ hours, until the beef is tender. Transfer the beef to a platter. Cover and keep warm. If using the anchovies, mince them and then mash them with a fork. Stir into the pan sauce in the slow cooker. Blend the flour with the butter and stir into the pan sauce. If cooking on LOW, increase the temperature setting to HIGH. Cover and cook, stirring 2 or 3 times, until the sauce is thickened, about 20 more minutes. Stir in the capers.

Return the beef to the slow cooker, spooning the sauce over the meat to evenly coat. Serve at once, sprinkling parsley on each portion, if using.

○ **PER SERVING:** 6 g carbohydrate (includes trace dietary fiber), 30 g protein, 22 g fat, 360 calories
○ **DIABETIC EXCHANGES:** ½ vegetable, 4 lean meat, 2 fat

Maria's Sunday Night Stew

When I lived in Southern California, I employed a Spanish-speaking housekeeper to help with the house and my young sons while I was producing wine and cooking shows. Maria loved to cook her native dishes. Because Sunday was her day off, she often left a pot of delicious food in the refrigerator for me to reheat for Sunday night supper. This stew was one of our favorites; she said it was a popular Sunday night meal at her home, too. Although Maria cooked the stew on top of the stove, it's easier to use a slow cooker.

Rinse the chicken breasts and pat dry. Cut into 1-inch pieces. Cut the beef into 1-inch pieces. Toss the chicken and steak with the lime juice, orange juice, all but 2 tablespoons of the cilantro, and the cumin. Place the mixture in the bottom of a 3½-quart or larger crockery slow cooker. Add the onion, scallions, bell pepper, and chiles. Combine the broth and tomato paste. Pour into the cooker.

Cover and cook on LOW for 7 to 9 hours or on HIGH for 3½ to 4½ hours. Add the pieces of corn during the last 20 minutes of cooking time if cooking on LOW (or last 10 minutes if cooking on HIGH).

Ladle the stew into individual dishes, allowing 1 piece of corn per serving. Sprinkle with the remaining cilantro and serve.

O **PER SERVING:** 13 g carbohydrate (includes 2 g dietary fiber), 27 g protein, 7 g fat, 216 calories

O **DIABETIC EXCHANGES:** 1½ vegetable, 3½ very lean meat, 1 fat

MAKES 6 SERVINGS

¾ pound boneless, skinless chicken breasts

¾ pound boneless lean beef chuck steak

3 tablespoons fresh lime juice

3 tablespoons fresh orange juice

½ cup minced fresh cilantro, divided

½ teaspoon ground cumin

1 large onion, finely chopped

6 scallions, finely chopped, including most of the green tops

1 medium red bell pepper, chopped

2 to 3 hot chiles, such as jalapeño or serrano, seeded and minced

1 (14½-ounce) can low-sodium beef broth

2 tablespoons tomato paste

1 large ear of fresh corn, shucked and cut into 1-inch rounds

Argentinean Beef Stew

MAKES 8 SERVINGS

2 pounds lean beef stew meat, trimmed of all fat

2 medium onions, chopped

2 cloves garlic, minced

1 tablespoon extra-virgin olive oil

2 medium tomatoes, seeded and chopped

2 pounds pumpkin, seeded, peeled, and cut into 1½-inch pieces

1 medium green bell pepper, chopped

1 medium red bell pepper, chopped

2 teaspoons crushed dried oregano

2 teaspoons crushed dried basil

1 teaspoon crushed dried thyme

1 teaspoon freshly ground pepper

½ cup dried apricot halves, coarsely chopped

1 (14½-ounce) can low-sodium beef broth

¼ cup dry sherry

This is a popular, hearty stew in Argentina, where beef reigns supreme. It works extremely well in a slow cooker. If you can find them, use Turkish dried apricots in this recipe—they're of superior quality. I buy mine from the bulk foods department of a local market, but you might need to look at natural foods stores.

Traditionally, this stew is served in a baked whole pumpkin, scooping out some of the pumpkin along with the stew. I put the pumpkin in the stew, but if you prefer the more elegant presentation, omit the pumpkin in the recipe and follow the directions given in the box opposite. Carbs are figured on ¼ cup of cooked pumpkin.

In a large nonstick skillet over medium-high heat, sauté the beef, onions, and garlic in the olive oil until the beef is browned, about 5 minutes. Drain off all fat.

Transfer the beef-onion mixture to the bottom of a 5-quart or larger crockery slow cooker. Add the tomatoes, pumpkin, bell peppers, oregano, basil, thyme, and pepper. Lay the apricots on top and pour in the broth and sherry. Cover and cook on LOW for 8 to 10 hours or on HIGH for 4 to 5 hours.

Ladle the stew into bowls and serve hot.

○ PER SERVING: 13 g carbohydrate (includes 2 g dietary fiber), 25 g protein, 10 g fat, 242 calories

○ DIABETIC EXCHANGES: ½ bread/starch, 1 vegetable, 3 lean meat, ½ fat

Sherried Beef and Mushrooms

I have been making this for more than twenty years, first in the oven and later in a crockery slow cooker, for which it is very suitable. The recipe makes a lot so it's quite wonderful for a potluck supper. Shiitake mushrooms, which weren't available when I first made this, are wonderful in this dish. To lower the fat even more, make this the day before; refrigerate overnight and skim the fat from the surface. Reheat the dish before serving.

MAKES 8 SERVINGS

3 pounds boneless beef chuck
    roast, trimmed of fat
1 pound shiitake mushrooms,
    cleaned, stems discarded,
    and caps sliced
6 cloves garlic, thinly sliced
1 envelope (1/2 of a 2.2-ounce
    package) dry onion soup
    mix
1/2 cup dry sherry
1/2 cup low-sodium canned beef
    broth

Cut the roast into 1-inch cubes. Combine the remaining ingredients with the beef in a 5-quart or larger crockery slow cooker, stirring gently to avoid breaking up the mushrooms.

Cover and cook on LOW for 8 to 10 hours or on HIGH for 4 to 5 hours, until the beef is tender. Serve hot.

O **PER SERVING:** 11 g carbohydrate (includes 1 g dietary fiber), 34 g protein, 12 g fat, 296 calories

O **DIABETIC EXCHANGES:** 2 vegetable, 4 1/2 lean meat

SERVING IN A PUMPKIN SHELL

Make the Argentinean beef stew as directed (see p.52), omitting the pieces of pumpkin. Instead, purchase a medium-large pumpkin. Cut off the top and remove the seeds and strings. Brush the inside of the pumpkin with butter and sprinkle lightly with salt and pepper. Fill the pumpkin with crumpled aluminum foil and bake at 325°F for 45 minutes to 1 hour, until the pumpkin is tender when pierced with a knife. Remove the foil and set the pumpkin in a shallow serving dish. Fill the pumpkin with the hot stew. When serving, scoop out some of the pumpkin along with the stew.

On Safari Three-Meat Stew

MAKES 8 SERVINGS

2 tablespoons all-purpose flour

1 teaspoon ground coriander

1 teaspoon ground cumin

1/2 teaspoon crushed dried oregano

1/4 teaspoon crushed dried thyme

1/4 teaspoon freshly ground pepper

1 pound lean beef stew meat, trimmed of fat

1/2 pound lean veal stew meat, trimmed of fat

1/2 pound lean lamb stew meat, trimmed of fat

1 tablespoon canola oil

2 large onions, thinly sliced

4 cloves garlic, minced

1 hot chile, such as jalapeño or serrano, seeded and minced

1 (14½-ounce) can whole plum tomatoes, including juice

1 (14½-ounce) can low-sodium beef broth

1½ cups Burgundy wine or additional broth

1 tablespoon white wine vinegar

1 pound fresh okra, stemmed

1/2 cup coarsely chopped roasted peanuts

Whenever my sister-in-law comes back from her travels all over the world, she's full of ideas for me to use in my cookbooks or on my website—usually not exact recipes, just ideas for combinations of foods and spices. Such was when she came back from a three-week safari to Kenya. After a day of game watching at Masai Mara, the cook served an earthy stew similar to this while everyone watched hippos cavorting in the river nearby.

Okra is native to Africa and is often called "ladies' fingers" because of its shape. The okra is added near the end of the cooking time so that it keeps its crunchy texture. The safari cook frequently used peanuts as an ingredient or garnish, calling them groundnuts.

Combine the flour, coriander, cumin, oregano, thyme, and pepper in a large resealable plastic bag. Add the beef, veal, and lamb. Shake well to evenly coat the meats with the flour mixture.

Heat the oil in a large nonstick skillet over medium-high heat. Add the meats and sauté, stirring frequently, until the meats are well browned on all sides, about 5 minutes.

Place the onions, garlic, and chile in the bottom of a 5-quart or larger crockery slow cooker. Add the meats to the cooker. Stir in the tomatoes with juice, the broth, and wine.

Cover and cook on LOW for 7½ to 9½ hours or on HIGH for 3½ to 4½ hours. Stir in the vinegar and okra. If cooking on LOW, increase the temperature setting to HIGH. Re-cover and cook 20 to 30 minutes, until the okra is just tender.

Ladle the stew into bowls and garnish each serving with a tablespoon of chopped peanuts. Serve hot.

○ PER SERVING: 15 g carbohydrate (includes 4 g dietary fiber), 32 g protein, 14 g fat, 323 calories

○ DIABETIC EXCHANGES: 2 vegetable, 2½ very lean meat, 1½ lean meat, 1½ fat

Parvine's Beef Stew

My friend Parvine Latimore is a marvelous cook, not only of her native Persian food, but also stick-to-your-ribs comfort food. After her last visit, my freezer was stocked with homey dishes such as this savory stew.

Place the onions in the bottom of a 5-quart or larger crockery slow cooker. Season the beef with salt and pepper and arrange on top of the onions. Add the green beans to the cooker, along with the tomatoes with juice and the broth.

Sprinkle with the Italian herb seasoning, basil, garlic powder, and paprika. Add the bay leaves.

Cover and cook on LOW for 6 to 8 hours or on HIGH for 3½ to 4 hours, until the beef is very tender. Discard the bay leaves. Ladle the stew into shallow soup bowls and serve.

○ PER SERVING: 15 g carbohydrate (includes 5 g dietary fiber), 45 g protein, 15 g fat, 378 calories
○ DIABETIC EXCHANGES: 3 vegetable, 6 lean meat, 2 fat

MAKES 8 SERVINGS

1 pound yellow onions, coarsely chopped

2½ pounds boneless beef top sirloin, trimmed of all fat and cubed

Salt and freshly ground pepper, to taste

1½ pounds fresh green beans, trimmed

1 (28-ounce) can diced tomatoes, including juice

1 cup low-sodium canned beef broth

1 heaping teaspoon crushed dried Italian herb seasoning

1 heaping teaspoon crushed dried basil

1 teaspoon garlic powder

½ teaspoon sweet paprika

2 bay leaves

Carne Guisada

MAKES 6 SERVINGS

1½ **pounds lean beef top round steak, trimmed and cut into thin strips**

Salt and freshly ground pepper, to taste

1 **medium onion, chopped**

3 **cloves garlic, minced**

2 **(10-ounce) cans chopped tomatoes with green chile peppers, including juice**

1 **teaspoon chili powder**

1 **teaspoon ground cumin**

1 **teaspoon crushed dried oregano**

2 **tablespoons chopped fresh cilantro**

Low-carb whole wheat flour tortillas (optional), warmed

This is a popular beef dish here in Texas and south of the border, where recipes vary from country to country. You can tuck this into low-carb tortillas for out-of-hand eating or spoon it over shredded lettuce to eat with a fork.

Season the beef strips with salt and pepper. Place in the bottom of a 3½-quart or larger crockery slow cooker. In a large bowl, combine the remaining ingredients *except* the cilantro and tortillas. Pour into the slow cooker.

Cover and cook on LOW for 7 to 9 hours or on HIGH for 3½ to 4½ hours. Just before serving, stir in the cilantro. If using, spoon the meat and vegetable mixture into warm tortillas. Roll and serve immediately.

○ PER SERVING (STEW ONLY): 6 g carbohydrate (includes 2 g dietary fiber), 41 g protein, 7 g fat, 263 calories
○ DIABETIC EXCHANGES: 1 vegetable, 6 very lean meat, 1 fat

Beef Carbonnade

Traditionally, this Belgian stew gets its flavor from caramelized onions and its rich color from dark Flemish beer. I've used a low-carb beer, which lightens the color, but the flavor will be much the same.

In a large nonstick skillet, sauté the bacon over medium-high heat until crisp. Using a slotted spoon, transfer the bacon pieces to a paper towel to drain. Set aside. Season the beef with salt and pepper.

Discard all but 1 tablespoon bacon drippings from the skillet. Add the beef to the skillet and sauté over medium-high heat, turning once, until the beef is browned, about 5 minutes. Place the beef in the bottom of a 3½-quart or larger crockery slow cooker.

Add the butter to the skillet and place over medium heat. When the butter is melted, add the onions and garlic. Sauté, stirring often, until the onions are nicely browned, about 7 minutes. Transfer the onions and garlic to the slow cooker. Add the vinegar to the skillet and swirl around to deglaze the pan, scraping up any browned bits with a wooden spoon. Add the bouillon cube, beer, Worcestershire sauce, brown sugar, mustard, and thyme to the skillet. Cook, stirring, for 2 minutes. Pour over the beef and onions.

Cover and cook on LOW for 7 to 9 hours or on HIGH for 3½ to 4 hours, until the beef is very tender. Using a slotted spoon, transfer the beef and onions to a heated serving platter. Stir the cornstarch mixture into the slow cooker and, if cooking on LOW, increase the temperature setting to HIGH. Cook, stirring, until the mixture bubbles and thickens to form a gravy. Cook, stirring, for another 2 minutes. Pour the gravy over the beef and serve at once.

○ PER SERVING: 10 g carbohydrate (includes 1 g dietary fiber), 36 g protein, 32 g fat, 490 calories
○ DIABETIC EXCHANGES: 1 vegetable, 5 lean meat, 4 fat

MAKES 6 SERVINGS

2 slices lean bacon, finely diced
1 (2½-pound) boneless beef chuck roast, well trimmed of fat and cut into 1-inch cubes
Salt and freshly ground pepper, to taste
1 tablespoon unsalted butter
2 medium onions, thinly sliced
2 cloves garlic, thinly sliced
1 tablespoon red wine vinegar
1 beef bouillon cube (makes 2 cups broth), crushed
1 cup low-carb light beer
1 tablespoon Worcestershire sauce
1 tablespoon dark brown sugar
1 tablespoon Dijon mustard
½ teaspoon crushed dried thyme
2 teaspoons cornstarch dissolved in 1 tablespoon cold water

Souper-Easy Beef and Mushroom Ragout

MAKES 6 SERVINGS

2 pounds boneless beef top
   round steak, trimmed of all
   fat and cut into 1-inch cubes
1 (10¾-ounce) can condensed
   cream of mushroom soup
1 (10¾-ounce) can condensed
   cream of celery soup
1 envelope (½ of a 2.2-ounce
   package) dry onion soup
   mix
1 pound fresh shiitake
   mushrooms, cleaned and
   sliced
1 cup Burgundy wine
¼ cup sour cream

This is a great dish to come home to after an afternoon of tennis, golf, or any outdoor activity. Steam a couple of low-carb vegetables such as broccoli and cauliflower, and dinner's done.

In a 3½-quart or larger crockery slow cooker, combine the beef, mushroom soup, celery soup, and onion soup mix.

Cover and cook on LOW for 7 to 8 hours or on HIGH for 3½ to 4 hours. If cooking on LOW, increase the temperature setting to HIGH. Stir in the mushrooms and wine. Re-cover and cook for another 30 minutes. Stir in the sour cream and cook, uncovered, for 5 minutes more. Serve hot.

○ PER SERVING: 23 g carbohydrate (2 g dietary fiber), 38 g protein, 25 g fat, 472 calories
○ DIABETIC EXCHANGES: ½ bread/starch, 2 vegetable, 4½ lean meat, 2½ fat

PEELING PEARL ONIONS

These tiny onions are easy to peel if you first cook them in boiling water for 1 minute. Rinse under running cold water. Using a small, sharp knife, trim off the bottom and the top of each onion and slip off the skin. To keep the onions intact during the long, slow cooking, score the trimmed top and bottom of each onion with a shallow ×.

Beef Bourguignon

This is the first "gourmet" dinner that I learned to cook after I arrived in Southern California with the ink on my college diploma still wet. It soon became standard fare for the first time I invited a date for a meal. My recipe hasn't changed all that much over the years, only now I fix it in a slow cooker.

In a large nonstick skillet over medium-high heat, sauté the bacon pieces until crisp. Drain on paper towels and refrigerate until needed. Drain all fat from the skillet and add the olive oil. In a bowl, combine the flour, cayenne, salt, and pepper. Sprinkle on all sides of the skillet and brown, turning occasionally, for 5 minutes.

Meanwhile, place the pearl onions and mushrooms in the bottom of a 4-quart or larger crockery slow cooker. Transfer the beef to the slow cooker. Add the onion, carrot, and garlic to the skillet. Cook, stirring, for 2 minutes. Add to the cooker and sprinkle with the marjoram and thyme. Pour the wine and broth over all.

Cover and cook on LOW for 7 to 9 hours or on HIGH for 3½ to 4 hours, until the beef is very tender. Transfer the beef and vegetables to a serving dish and keep warm. If a thicker sauce is desired and if cooking on LOW, increase the temperature setting to HIGH. Whisk the dissolved cornstarch into the cooker and cook, stirring occasionally, until thickened, about 10 minutes. Ladle the sauce over the beef and vegetables and sprinkle with the parsley and reserved bacon. Serve immediately.

○ PER SERVING: 11 g carbohydrate (includes 1 g dietary fiber), 35 g protein, 13 g fat, 313 calories

○ DIABETIC EXCHANGES: 2 vegetable, 5 very lean meat, 2 fat

MAKES 6 SERVINGS

3 slices lean bacon, cut into 1-inch pieces

1 tablespoon extra-virgin olive oil

2 tablespoons all-purpose flour

⅛ teaspoon cayenne pepper

Salt and freshly ground black pepper, to taste

2 pounds boneless beef bottom round, trimmed of all fat and cut into 1½-inch pieces

8 ounces pearl onions, peeled (see page 58)

8 ounces white button mushrooms, cleaned

1 large onion, chopped

1 medium carrot, peeled and chopped

1 clove garlic, minced

½ teaspoon crushed dried marjoram

½ teaspoon crushed dried thyme

1¼ cups Burgundy wine

½ cup canned low-sodium beef broth

2 tablespoons cornstarch, dissolved in 2 tablespoons water (optional)

¼ cup chopped parsley

Curried Pork Stew

MAKES 6 SERVINGS

8 ounces pearl onions, peeled (see page 58)

2 cloves garlic, minced

1 large green bell pepper, cut into 1-inch pieces

1 large sweet potato (about 8 ounces), peeled and cut into 1-inch pieces

1 tablespoon curry powder, or to taste

$\frac{1}{2}$ teaspoon ground allspice

$\frac{1}{2}$ teaspoon crushed dried thyme

$\frac{1}{8}$ teaspoon ground cinnamon

2 pounds boneless pork tenderloin, cut into 1-inch pieces

1 (14$\frac{1}{2}$-ounce) can low-sodium chicken broth

1 bay leaf

Sweet potatoes naturally thicken this rich, curried stew. Put this stew on to cook early in the day of your first snowfall or cold snap to have an especially warming one-dish meal ready when the family gathers for supper.

Place the onions, garlic, bell pepper, and sweet potato in the bottom of a 3½-quart or larger crockery slow cooker. Combine the curry powder, allspice, thyme, and cinnamon. Sprinkle over the pork and toss to evenly coat. Add the pork to the cooker. Pour in the chicken broth and add the bay leaf.

Cover and cook on LOW for 8 to 10 hours or on HIGH for 4 to 5 hours. Discard the bay leaf. Ladle the stew into bowls and serve hot.

○ **PER SERVING:** 11 g carbohydrate (includes 2 g dietary fiber), 36 g protein, 10 g fat, 285 calories

○ **DIABETIC EXCHANGES:** ½ bread/starch, ½ vegetable, 4½ lean meat

Fireside Stew

This is the kind of meal that's perfect for dining in front of a roaring fire, oblivious to the raging winter storm outside. I would serve this in a shallow soup plate with a dollop of creamy polenta alongside.

Place the onion and garlic in the bottom of a 3½-quart or larger crockery slow cooker. Top with the chiles and bell pepper.

In a resealable plastic bag, combine the flour, chili powder, cumin, pepper, oregano, and thyme. Add the pork and shake to coat evenly. Place the pork over the vegetables. Top with the tomatillos and tomatoes with juice. Combine the broth, wine, and tomato paste. Pour into the slow cooker. Do not stir.

Cover and cook on LOW for 8½ to 9½ hours or on HIGH for 4½ to 4½ hours. Add the zucchini and stir the stew. If cooking on LOW, increase the temperature setting to HIGH. Recover and cook for another 15 minutes. Ladle the stew into shallow soup bowls. Add a dollop of polenta alongside, if using.

○ PER SERVING (STEW ONLY): 23 g carbohydrate (includes 4 g dietary fiber), 30 g protein, 8 g fat, 282 calories
○ DIABETIC EXCHANGES: 4 vegetable, 3 lean meat

MAKES 4 SERVINGS

1 large onion, chopped

2 cloves garlic, minced

1 Anaheim chile, seeded and minced

1 jalapeño chile, seeded and minced

1 large red bell pepper, chopped

2 tablespoons all-purpose flour

1 teaspoon chili powder

½ teaspoon ground cumin

½ teaspoon freshly ground black pepper

½ teaspoon crushed dried oregano

½ teaspoon crushed dried thyme

1 pound lean boneless pork tenderloin, trimmed of fat and cut into 1-inch cubes

4 tomatillos, husked, rinsed, and coarsely chopped

1 (14½-ounce) can Italian plum tomatoes, including juice

1 cup canned low-sodium beef broth

½ cup dry red wine

2 tablespoons tomato paste

2 medium zucchini, halved lengthwise and cut into 1-inch slices

Creamy Polenta (see page 62; optional)

Creamy Polenta

MAKES 8 SERVINGS

1 quart water

Dash salt

1 cup instant polenta or stone-
  ground yellow cornmeal

2 tablespoons freshly grated
  Parmesan cheese

1 tablespoon unsalted butter

You'll find lots of uses for this delicious cornmeal mixture. Serve it hot from the stove or pour the mixture into a buttered square pan to cool completely. Then cut into squares or triangles and grill or sauté in a bit of olive oil.

Bring the water and salt to a rapid boil in a 2-quart saucepan over medium-high heat. Sprinkle the polenta over the boiling water. Reduce the heat to medium and cook, stirring constantly, until the polenta is thick and creamy, about 5 minutes. Stir in the Parmesan cheese and butter.

○ **PER SERVING:** 18 g carbohydrate (includes 2 g dietary fiber), 3 g protein, 2 g fat, 98 calories

○ **DIABETIC EXCHANGES:** 1 bread/starch, ½ fat

Thai Pork and Pineapple Stew

Everybody seems to love Thai food these days. Frequently the dishes are cooked with kaffir lime leaves, which are hard to find. I've substituted fresh lime juice and lime zest with good results in this pork stew. The Thai seasoning is made by several companies and usually found in the spice aisle of a well-stocked supermarket. Cooking the stew in a crockery slow cooker makes this a super-easy dish for entertaining family or friends.

Heat the oil in a large nonstick skillet over medium-high heat. Add the pork and brown on all sides, about 6 minutes total. Place the bell peppers in the bottom of a 3½-quart or larger crockery slow cooker. Add the pork and any pan drippings.

Place the broth, lime zest and lime juice, garlic, soy sauce, brown sugar, and Thai seasoning in a 2-cup measuring cup. Add enough water to make 2 cups. Mix with a fork and pour into the slow cooker.

Cover and cook on LOW for 7 to 8 hours or on HIGH for 3½ to 4 hours. Add the pineapple and, if cooking on LOW, increase the temperature setting to HIGH. Re-cover and cook for 30 to 40 minutes, until the pineapple is tender.

Ladle the stew into shallow bowls. Sprinkle each serving with some of the scallions, basil, and a scant tablespoon of the cashews. Serve hot.

○ PER SERVING: 15 g carbohydrate (includes 1 g dietary fiber), 35 g protein, 14 g fat, 325 calories
○ DIABETIC EXCHANGES: ½ fruit, ½ vegetable, 4½ lean meat, 1 fat

MAKES 6 SERVINGS

2 teaspoons canola oil

2 pounds boneless pork tenderloin, cut into 1-inch cubes

1 medium red bell pepper, cut into julienne strips

1 medium yellow bell pepper, cut into julienne strips

1 cup canned low-sodium chicken broth

Grated zest and juice of 1 lime

3 cloves garlic, minced

2 tablespoons reduced-sodium soy sauce

1 tablespoon light brown sugar

1 teaspoon Thai seasoning

2 cups cubed fresh pineapple

2 scallions, white part and 1 inch green, chopped

2 tablespoons chopped fresh basil

¼ cup roasted cashews

Tuscan Pork Ragout

MAKES 4 SERVINGS

1 tablespoon extra-virgin olive
    oil
2 pounds lean boneless pork
    shoulder, trimmed and cut
    into 1-inch cubes
1 medium onion, diced
2 cloves garlic, minced
1/2 teaspoon crushed dried
    thyme
1/4 teaspoon crushed dried
    rosemary
1/4 teaspoon crushed dried sage
1/8 teaspoon ground cinnamon
1/8 teaspoon ground cloves
1 cup canned low-sodium
    chicken broth
2 tablespoons balsamic vinegar
2 tablespoons red wine vinegar
2 tablespoons tomato paste
Cooked low-carb pasta
    (optional)
3 strips bacon, cooked crisp and
    crumbled
3 tablespoons minced fresh
    flat-leaf parsley

This is the essence of Tuscan cooking—a long-simmered stew cooked until the meat falls apart, richly flavored with herbs and spices. Toss this with some low-carb pasta, add a leafy green salad, light a candle or two, and you're ready to dine in style.

Heat the oil in a large nonstick skillet over medium-high heat; add the pork and brown on all sides, about 5 minutes total.

In the bottom of a 3½-quart or larger crockery slow cooker, combine the onion, garlic, thyme, rosemary, sage, cinnamon, and cloves. Place the pork on top. In a large glass measuring cup, combine the chicken broth, both vinegars, and tomato paste. Pour over the pork.

Cover and cook on LOW for 7 to 9 hours or on HIGH for 3½ to 4½ hours, until the pork is very tender. If using, serve over low-carb pasta, sprinkled with the bacon and parsley.

○ **PER SERVING (RAGOUT ONLY):** 8 g carbohydrate (includes 1 g dietary fiber), 41 g protein, 26 g fat, 436 calories
○ **DIABETIC EXCHANGES:** 1 vegetable, 6 lean meat, 2 fat

Stifado

A Greek way of braising or stewing in red wine and red wine vinegar with spices, stifado is perfect for slow cookers. This particular version is similar to one that I enjoyed in on the island of Corfu. There it was made with lamb, but you could also use beef or veal.

Place the onions and garlic in the bottom of a 3½-quart or larger crockery slow cooker. Toss the lamb with the flour and place on top of the onions. Drain the tomatoes, reserving the juice. Coarsely chop the tomatoes and place over the lamb.

In a measuring cup, combine the wine, vinegar, and tomato paste. Add enough of the reserved tomato juice to make 1 cup. Whisk in the allspice and pour over the lamb mixture. Submerge the bay leaves and cinnamon stick.

Cover and cook on LOW for 7 to 9 hours, until the lamb is tender. Discard the bay leaves and cinnamon stick. Transfer the lamb, vegetables, and some of the pan juices to a heated serving dish. Serve immediately.

O PER SERVING: 23 g carbohydrate (includes 1 dietary fiber), 34 g protein, 8 g fat, 313 calories

O DIABETIC EXCHANGES: 3½ vegetable, 4½ lean meat

MAKES 6 SERVINGS

1½ pounds small white pearl
onions, peeled (see page 58)

2 cloves garlic, minced

1½ pounds lean lamb, beef, or
veal, trimmed of fat and cut
into 1½-inch pieces

2 tablespoons all-purpose flour

1 (14½-ounce) can whole plum
tomatoes

½ cup dry red wine

¼ cup red wine vinegar

2 tablespoons tomato paste

¼ teaspoon ground allspice

2 bay leaves

1 (3-inch) cinnamon stick

French Lamb Stew

MAKES 6 SERVINGS

2 pounds boneless lamb
   shoulder or leg, trimmed of
   fat and cut into 1-inch cubes
Salt and freshly ground pepper,
   to taste
1 tablespoon *herbes de Provence*
   (see page 67)
1 teaspoon Hungarian paprika
2 tablespoons extra-virgin olive
   oil
1 medium onion, chopped
1 medium sweet potato, peeled
   and diced
1 medium carrot, peeled and
   chopped
3 cloves garlic, minced
1 cup dry red wine
1½ cups canned low-sodium
   beef broth
12 ounces fresh sugar snap
   peas, trimmed

Stew is a great dish for entertaining; the slow cooker crockery insert can go right to the buffet table, keeping the food hot. I would serve this lovely lamb stew in a shallow bowl over a wholesome grain such as spelt, followed with a field greens salad with grape tomatoes and a fresh chive vinaigrette. Dessert could be as simple as fresh fruit and cheese.

Season the lamb with salt and pepper. Combine the *herbes de Provence* and paprika. Sprinkle over the lamb and toss to evenly coat. In a large nonstick skillet, heat the oil over medium–high heat. Add the lamb and cook, stirring, until well browned, about 5 minutes total. Using a slotted spoon, transfer the lamb to the bottom of a 3½–quart or larger crockery slow cooker. Top with the onion, sweet potato, carrot, and garlic. Pour in the wine and broth.

Cover and cook on LOW for 8 to 10 hours or on HIGH for 4 to 5 hours. Just before serving, cook the sugar snap peas in boiling water on top of the stove until just crisp tender, 3 to 4 minutes. Drain well and stir into the stew. Serve immediately.

○ PER SERVING: 9 g carbohydrate (includes 2 g dietary fiber), 37 g protein, 28 g fat, 449 calories
○ DIABETIC EXCHANGES: 2 vegetable, 5 lean meat, 3 fat

Herbes de Provence

Market stalls in Provence sell a mixture of dried herbs called herbes de Provence *which are sometimes packaged in little cloth sacks, plastic bags, or, as more commonly found in the United States, tiny clay crocks. You can make your own for a fraction of the cost of those you'd buy in a specialty shop.*

Mix to a fine powder in a food processor or blender. Transfer to an airtight container and store away from light and heat. Use within 3 months.

MAKES ABOUT 7 TABLESPOONS

2 tablespoons dried basil

4 teaspoons dried oregano

2 teaspoons dried marjoram

2 teaspoons dried thyme

1 teaspoon dried sage

1 teaspoon dried mint

1 teaspoon dried rosemary

1 teaspoon fennel seed

1 teaspoon dried lavender (optional)

Lamb Tagine

MAKES 6 SERVINGS

1 medium onion, grated

6 cloves garlic, chopped

1 (2-pound) boneless lamb
  shoulder roast, trimmed of
  all fat

¹/₂ cup canned low-sodium beef
  broth

1 tablespoon grated fresh
  ginger

¹/₄ teaspoon cayenne pepper

¹/₄ teaspoon ground cinnamon

¹/₈ teaspoon crushed saffron
  threads

1 (14¹/₂-ounce) can crushed
  tomatoes

¹/₂ cup chopped red onion

1¹/₄ pounds fresh okra, tops
  trimmed

¹/₄ cup chopped fresh cilantro

A restaurant in Fort Worth, Texas, serves a similar lamb tagine, which is slow-roasted in the oven in a covered clay casserole. The first time I tried fixing it in a slow cooker, the okra was overdone, but on subsequent testing, it was wonderful when the okra and tomatoes were added near the end of the cooking time. This is a superb way to prepare a lamb shoulder roast.

Place the grated onion and garlic in the bottom of a 3½-quart or larger crockery slow cooker. Place the lamb on top of the onion, cutting the roast if necessary to fit into the slow cooker.

In a large bowl, combine the broth, ginger, cayenne, cinnamon, and saffron. Pour over the roast.

Cover and cook on LOW for 10 to 12 hours or on HIGH for 5 to 6 hours. About 30 minutes (20 minutes if cooking on HIGH) before cooking is complete, add the tomatoes and red onion to a large nonstick skillet over medium heat. Once the tomatoes start to bubble, add the okra and cilantro. Cover and simmer for 10 minutes. Spoon the tomato-okra mixture over the lamb in the slow cooker, re-cover, and cook for another 20 minutes on LOW or 10 minutes on HIGH.

Transfer the lamb to a carving board. Keep the vegetables and pan juices warm. Slice the lamb and arrange on a large, heated serving platter. Spoon the vegetables and pan juices around the lamb. Serve immediately.

○ **PER SERVING:** 15 g carbohydrate (includes 2 g dietary fiber), 38 g protein, 24 g fat, 422 calories

○ **DIABETIC EXCHANGES:** 2¹/₂ vegetable, 5 lean meat, 2 fat

Caribbean Fish Stew

Some of the most memorable fish dishes that I've enjoyed on my travels have been the fish stews found throughout the Caribbean—just bursting with native fresh fish, okra, onions, tomatoes, and hot chiles. I can buy Scotch Bonnet chiles at my local grocer, but you may need to substitute habanero or Thai chiles.

In a large nonstick skillet, sauté the Canadian bacon in the olive oil over medium heat for 4 to 5 minutes, stirring occasionally. Using a slotted spoon, transfer the bacon to a 4-quart or larger crockery slow cooker. Add the onion, bell pepper, and garlic to the skillet. Sauté, stirring occasionally, until the vegetables are limp, 4 minutes. Transfer the vegetables to the slow cooker. Top with the okra, chiles, and bay leaf. Sprinkle with the thyme and cayenne. Add the tomatoes with juice, clam juice, and broth.

Cover and cook on LOW for 6 to 7 hours or on HIGH for 3 to 3½ hours, until all the vegetables are tender. If cooking on LOW, increase cooking temperature to HIGH.

Rinse the snapper and cut crosswise into ½-inch strips. Rinse the scallops and cut each one in half. Peel and devein the shrimp. Cut each shrimp in half lengthwise. Stir the fish and seafood into the slow cooker. Cook, covered, until the fish flakes easily with a fork, the scallops are firm, and the shrimp are pink and firm, about 15 minutes. Stir in the orange zest and cilantro. Discard the bay leaf. Ladle the stew into hot soup bowls and pass the hot sauce separately for sprinkling onto each serving, as desired.

○ PER SERVING: 18 g carbohydrate (includes 2 g dietary fiber), 56 g protein, 6 g fat, 362 calories

○ DIABETIC EXCHANGES: 3 vegetable, 7½ very lean meat, ½ fat

MAKES 6 SERVINGS

2 ounces Canadian bacon, cut into thin strips

2 teaspoons extra-virgin olive oil

1 large onion, cut into 1-inch pieces

1 large red bell pepper, cut into 1-inch pieces

3 cloves garlic, minced

1 pound fresh okra, tops trimmed

1 to 2 Scotch Bonnet chiles, seeded and minced, (see recipe headnote)

1 bay leaf

2 teaspoons crushed dried thyme

½ teaspoon cayenne pepper, or to taste

1 (28-ounce) can plum tomatoes, including juice

2 cups bottled clam juice

2 cups canned low-sodium chicken broth

1 pound red snapper fillets, skinned

1 pound sea scallops

1 pound large shrimp, shells on

1 tablespoon grated orange zest

¼ cup coarsely chopped fresh cilantro

Bottle of Caribbean hot sauce, for passing

North Beach Cioppino

MAKES 6 SERVINGS

2 teaspoons extra-virgin olive oil

2 medium onions, chopped

1 medium green bell pepper, diced

1 medium bulb fennel, trimmed and diced

2 cloves garlic, minced

4 cups bottled clam juice

1 cup dry red wine or additional water

1 (28-ounce) can crushed Italian tomatoes

2 tablespoons tomato paste

1 teaspoon crushed dried basil

1 teaspoon crushed dried oregano

$\frac{1}{2}$ teaspoon red pepper flakes

$\frac{1}{2}$ teaspoon crushed dried thyme

1 bay leaf

1 pound sea bass or red snapper fillets

1 pound medium shrimp, shells on

$\frac{1}{2}$ cup chopped fresh parsley

Salt and freshly ground pepper, to taste

$\frac{1}{2}$ cup freshly grated Parmesan cheese

$\frac{1}{4}$ cup chopped scallions, white part and 2 inches green

Years ago, I traveled frequently from Los Angeles to San Francisco to meet with various food clients. On one such trip I was invited to a houseboat party, where I was promised that I'd learn to make cioppino, the legendary fish stew that's served at countless Italian restaurants in the city by the Bay. I attended, took notes, and became addicted to this savory dish. The recipe adapts beautifully to preparation in a slow cooker.

Heat the oil in a large skillet over medium-high heat. Add the onions, bell pepper, fennel, and garlic. Sauté until the vegetables are limp, about 5 minutes. Transfer the mixture to a 3½-quart or larger crockery slow cooker. Stir in the clam juice, wine, tomatoes, tomato paste, basil, oregano, red pepper flakes, thyme, and bay leaf.

Cover and cook on LOW for 4 to 5 hours. Rinse the sea bass and cut into 1-inch squares. Peel and devein the shrimp. Increase the cooking temperature to HIGH and add the sea bass and shrimp. Cover and cook until the fish is cooked through and the shrimp are firm and pink, about 15 minutes. Discard the bay leaf and stir in the parsley. Taste and add salt and pepper as needed. Ladle into large soup bowls and sprinkle each serving with the cheese and scallions. Serve immediately.

○ PER SERVING: 18 g carbohydrate (includes 4 g dietary fiber), 37 g protein, 7 g fat, 283 calories

○ DIABETIC EXCHANGES: 3 vegetable, $\frac{1}{2}$ very lean meat, $4\frac{1}{2}$ lean meat, $\frac{1}{2}$ fat

Winter Vegetable Stew

This is a versatile, warming stew made from ingredients you're likely to already have on hand. To make the dish visually attractive, cut the vegetables into large pieces. With the all-day slow cooking, it'll be done to perfection by dinnertime.

Remember this dish when you're broiling fish or chicken.

In a 5-quart or larger crockery slow cooker, arrange all of the vegetables *except* the cabbage in the order given. In a large measuring cup, combine the broth, soy sauce, lemon juice, thyme, and rosemary. Pour over the vegetables; do not stir.

Cover and cook on LOW for 8 to 10 hours or on HIGH for 4 to 5 hours. If cooking on LOW, increase the cooking temperature to HIGH and add the cabbage. Re-cover and cook for another 30 minutes, until the vegetables are tender. Transfer the vegetables and some of the cooking broth to a heated serving dish. Serve hot.

○ PER SERVING: 18 g carbohydrate (includes 3 g dietary fiber), 5 g protein, 1 g fat, 87 calories

○ DIABETIC EXCHANGES: 3 vegetable

MAKES 6 SERVINGS

3 medium carrots, peeled, cut in half lengthwise, and cut into 3-inch lengths

3 medium ribs celery, cut into 3-inch lengths

1 medium onion, cut into eighths

3 cloves garlic, quartered

6 ounces firm button mushrooms, cleaned and quartered

6 medium plum tomatoes, cut in half lengthwise

1¼ cups canned low-sodium chicken broth

2 tablespoons reduced-sodium soy sauce

1 tablespoon fresh lemon juice

1 teaspoon crushed dried thyme

¼ teaspoon crushed dried rosemary

1 small head cabbage, cored and cut into 6 wedges

Hot and Spicy Chili

MAKES 6 SERVINGS

1 pound chorizo, casings
  discarded
1 medium onion, chopped
1 (1.2-ounce) package chili
  seasoning mix
1 (10-ounce) can diced tomatoes
  with green chiles, including
  juice
1 (15-ounce) can Mexican-style
  chili beans, undrained
¼ cup water
½ cup sour cream
⅓ cup shredded sharp cheddar
  cheese

Just six items and a couple of condiments are needed to create this satisfying meal. Serve steaming bowls of this special chili with a dollop of sour cream on top to deflect some of the fiery heat. If your market doesn't carry chorizo sausage, substitute Cajun andouille or a hot pork sausage.

In a large nonstick skillet over medium heat, brown the chorizo and onion until the sausage is no longer pink, about 5 minutes. Transfer to a 3½-quart or larger crockery slow cooker and stir in the seasoning mix, tomatoes with juice, undrained beans, and water.

Cover and cook on LOW for 4 to 6 hours or on HIGH for 2 to 3 hours. Ladle into soup bowls and place a dollop of sour cream on top of each serving. Sprinkle with the cheese and serve.

O **PER SERVING:** 21 g carbohydrate (includes 4 g dietary fiber), 25 g protein, 36 g fat, 511 calories
O **DIABETIC EXCHANGES:** 1 vegetable, 3 lean meat, 6 fat

Pork and Black Bean Chili

You can't have too many chili recipes in your cooking repertoire; most everyone loves a good bowl of chili.

In a large, heavy saucepan over medium-low heat, sauté the onion and garlic in the olive oil until the onion is wilted, about 5 minutes. Stir in the chili powder, oregano, cumin, tomatoes with juice, black beans, and tomato paste. Transfer the mixture to a 3½-quart or larger crockery slow cooker and stir in the pork cubes and beef broth.

Cover and cook on LOW for 7 to 8 hours or on HIGH for 3½ to 4 hours. Divide the chili into 4 shallow soup bowls. Sprinkle each serving with 1 tablespoon of the cheese and dollop each with 1 tablespoon of the sour cream.

O PER SERVING: 34 g carbohydrate (includes 9 g dietary fiber), 38 g protein, 13 g fat, 392 calories
O DIABETIC EXCHANGES: 1 bread/starch, 3 vegetable, 3½ lean meat, 1 fat

MAKES 4 SERVINGS

1 medium onion, cut in half and thinly sliced

2 cloves garlic, minced

2 to 3 teaspoons good-quality chili powder

1 teaspoon crushed dried oregano

1 teaspoon ground cumin

1 (14½-ounce) can diced tomatoes, including juice

1 (15-ounce) can black beans, drained and rinsed

1 (6-ounce) can tomato paste

1 pound boneless pork tenderloin, trimmed of fat and cubed

1 (14-ounce) can low-sodium beef broth

¼ cup shredded Monterey Jack cheese

¼ cup sour cream

Texas Bowl of Red

MAKES 10 SERVINGS

4 pounds ground beef round

2 large onions, chopped

6 cloves garlic, minced

2 jalapeño chiles, seeded and
   minced

2 tablespoons chili powder

2 teaspoons crushed dried
   oregano, preferably Mexican

1 teaspoon ground cumin

3 (14½-ounce) cans whole
   tomatoes, coarsely chopped,
   including juice

1 (10-ounce) can chopped
   tomatoes with green chiles,
   including juice

1 (6-ounce) can tomato paste

1½ cups canned low-sodium
   beef broth

Topping

1¼ cups sour cream

⅓ cup chopped fresh cilantro

2 teaspoons chili powder

½ teaspoon onion powder

⅛ teaspoon cayenne pepper

Although here in Texas chili is likely to be made with venison, I prefer to use lean ground beef. This makes a lot so it's perfect when you have friends over to watch the big game. Make sure your chili powder is of good quality and fresh.

In a large nonstick skillet over medium-high heat, sauté the beef, onions, garlic, and chiles, stirring often to break up any lumps, until the beef is no longer pink, about 5 minutes. Drain off excess fat. Using a slotted spoon, transfer the mixture to a 5-quart or larger crockery slow cooker. Stir in the chili powder, oregano, cumin, tomatoes with juice, the tomato paste, and broth.

Cover and cook on LOW for 8 to 10 hours or on HIGH for 4 to 5 hours. In the meantime, mix together the topping ingredients and place in a serving bowl.

Ladle the chili into bowls and pass the topping for spooning on top.

○ PER SERVING: 11 g carbohydrate (includes 2 g dietary fiber), 42 g protein, 28 g fat, 472 calories

○ DIABETIC EXCHANGES: 2 vegetable, 6 lean meat, 2½ fat

Chili Soup

My brother, Laile, loves to make soup in the slow cooker. His recipe is particularly appropriate when small children are in attendance, as it has a mild chili flavor. Pass a shaker of crushed red pepper flakes so that those who prefer more spice can add it at the table.

In a large nonstick skillet over medium-high heat, sauté the beef, onion, and bell pepper, stirring often to break up any lumps, until the beef is no longer pink, about 5 minutes. Drain off the excess fat. Transfer the mixture to a 3½-quart or larger crockery slow cooker. Stir in the tomato sauce, tomatoes with juice, beans, chili powder, garlic powder, oregano, cumin, and water.

Cover and cook on LOW for 7 to 8 hours or on HIGH for 3½ to 4 hours. Ladle into soup bowls and top each serving with 2 tablespoons sour cream, 2 tablespoons cheese, and a scattering of scallions. Serve immediately. If using, pass the red pepper flakes separately to sprinkle on each serving.

O PER SERVING: 24 g carbohydrate (includes 6 g dietary fiber), 39 g protein, 18 g fat, 404 calories
O DIABETIC EXCHANGES: ½ bread/starch, 2 vegetable, 4½ very lean meat, 2½ fat

MAKES 6 SERVINGS

2 pounds lean ground beef sirloin or ground turkey
1 medium onion, chopped
1 medium green bell pepper, chopped
1 (8-ounce) can tomato sauce
1 (14½-ounce) can stewed tomatoes, including juice
1 (15-ounce) can pinto beans, drained and rinsed
2 teaspoons chili powder
1 teaspoon garlic powder
1 teaspoon crushed dried oregano
½ teaspoon ground cumin
2 cups water
¾ cup sour cream
¾ cup shredded cheddar cheese
1 bunch scallions, white part and 1 inch green, chopped
Crushed dried red pepper flakes, for sprinkling (optional)

White Chili

MAKES 8 SERVINGS

3 pounds boneless, skinless
  chicken breast halves

1 tablespoon canola oil

6 medium fresh tomatillos,
  husked and chopped

2 medium onions, chopped

3 cloves garlic, minced

1 (4-ounce) can chipotle chiles
  in adobo sauce, cut into thin
  strips

1 tablespoon ground cumin

2 teaspoons crushed dried
  oregano

1/4 teaspoon cayenne pepper

4 cups canned low-sodium
  chicken broth

1 (15-ounce) can Great Northern
  white beans, drained and
  rinsed

1 cup sliced pickled okra, for
  garnish (optional)

1/2 cup finely chopped red
  onion, for garnish (optional)

3/4 cup sour cream, for garnish
  (optional)

This is a great chili to take to a potluck supper. Offer sliced pickled okra, chopped red onion, and sour cream as condiments to top the steaming bowls of chili.

Rinse the chicken; discard all fat. Pat the chicken dry with paper towels. Cut into 1-inch pieces. Heat the oil in a large nonstick skillet over medium-high heat. Add the chicken and brown on all sides, stirring frequently, about 5 minutes.

Meanwhile, place the tomatillos, onions, and garlic in the bottom of a 5-quart or larger crockery slow cooker. Using a slotted spoon, transfer the chicken to the slow cooker. In a large measuring cup, combine the chipotle chiles and their sauce, the cumin, oregano, cayenne, and broth. Pour over the chicken.

Cover and cook on LOW 7 to 8 hours or on HIGH for 3½ to 4 hours. Stir in the beans. If cooking on LOW, increase the temperature setting to HIGH. Re-cover and cook for another 15 minutes. Ladle into bowls. If using, place the okra, red onion, and sour cream in individual serving bowls. Offer as toppings for the chili.

○ PER SERVING (CHILI ONLY): 14 g carbohydrate (includes 5 g dietary fiber), 38 g protein, 6 g fat, 277 calories

○ DIABETIC EXCHANGES: ½ bread/starch, 1 vegetable, 5 very lean meat, ½ fat

Lentil-Tomato Chili

This chili is high in carbs, but they are the good kind—rich in fiber and a good source of iron and phosphorus.

Crumble the ground sirloin into a large nonstick skillet. Sauté over medium-high heat, stirring often to break up any lumps, until the beef is no longer pink, about 8 minutes. Using a slotted spoon, transfer the beef to the bottom of a 3½-quart crockery slow cooker. Stir in the onion, garlic, lentils, tomatoes with juice, tomato paste, water, and wine. Season with the chilli powder, cumin, red pepper flakes, salt, and black pepper. Using the back of a wooden spoon, coarsely break up the tomatoes.

Cover and cook on LOW for 10 to 12 hours or on HIGH for 5 to 6 hours. Stir in the cilantro and ladle into heated soup bowls. Dollop 1 tablespoon sour cream on top of each serving and sprinkle with the avocado and a few cilantro leaves. Serve immediately.

○ PER SERVING: 31 g carbohydrate (includes 11 g dietary fiber), 23 g protein, 7 g fat, 270 calories
○ DIABETIC EXCHANGES: 1½ bread/starch, 1½ vegetable, 2 very lean protein, 1 fat

MAKES 12 SERVINGS

1½ pounds ground beef sirloin
1 large red onion, chopped
2 cloves garlic, minced
1 pound dried lentils, rinsed, drained, and picked over
1 (28-ounce) can peeled plum tomatoes, including juice
1 (6-ounce) can tomato paste
3 cups water
½ cup full-bodied dry red wine
4 teaspoons chili powder, or to taste
1 teaspoon ground cumin
¼ teaspoon crushed hot red pepper flakes
Salt and freshly ground black pepper, to taste
¼ cup chopped fresh cilantro, plus extra leaves for garnish
½ cup sour cream
1 large Hass avocado, peeled, pitted, and diced

Tempting Low-Carb Poultry from a Slow Cooker

THESE DAYS, AMERICANS EAT more poultry than red meat. Although a slow cooker does a great job cooking poultry, you need to be careful to avoid overcooking it. If you've been using your slow cooker for years, you may note that the cooking times given for the recipes in this book are considerably less than times given in your older recipes. Gone are the dry, overcooked pieces of chicken. There are lots of poultry recipes in this book—plenty to please every taste.

Chicken

Cooking a whole chicken is awkward, as it won't fit comfortably in a 3½-quart cooker. It has to be tilted at an angle. That is why most people who do a lot of crockery cooking have invested in a second, larger cooker. If you plan to do a lot of whole chickens, an oval model would be your best choice.

Chicken parts are easier to accommodate in a slow cooker, and grocers frequently have terrific sales on chicken parts, boneless, skinless chicken breasts, and bone-in and boneless chicken thighs. Because white meat cooks faster than dark, take care not to overcook the breast. It'll probably take no longer than 4½ to 5 hours, depending on the size. If you're cooking both white and dark meat, place the dark meat into the cooker first, then the white meat. That way as the cooking liquid starts to heat, the dark meat will start to cook and the white meat will catch up once the steam begins to build up.

Turkey

Turkey breasts and thighs both come out perfect in a slow cooker. You'll agree that turkey is not just for Thanksgiving when you try the recipes for Roasted Turkey Breast Stuffed with Herbs, Prosciutto, and Cheese, Turkey Tonnato with Arugula and Orange Slices, Turkey Meatballs Alfredo, or Barbecued Turkey Thighs.

Duck

I've also included an easy recipe for whole duck with oranges and almonds, which with a short period of oven roasting at the end produces the golden brown, crispy skin that we all associate with duck.

Slow-Roasted Chicken with Rosemary and Orange

MAKES 6 SERVINGS

1 (4-pound) whole roaster-fryer
   chicken
10 cloves garlic, peeled
2 tablespoons minced fresh
   rosemary plus 3 rosemary
   sprigs
1 large navel orange
¼ cup dry white wine
1 tablespoon balsamic vinegar

Roasted chicken is so delicious when prepared in this manner—redolent with fresh rosemary and the best of the season's navel oranges. You can cook the chicken with the skin on, but to keep the fat grams down, remove it before eating.

Remove and discard the giblets and neck from the chicken. Rinse the chicken and remove all excess fat from the neck and body cavities.

Mince 5 of the garlic cloves. Add the minced rosemary. Zest the orange to make 1 tablespoon zest. Add to the garlic-rosemary mixture. Starting from the neck cavity, with your fingers gently separate the skin from the breast meat without tearing the skin. Rub the garlic mixture under the loosened skin. Place the remaining whole garlic cloves and the rosemary sprigs in the body cavity. Place a wire rack or metal trivet in a 5-quart or larger crockery slow cooker. Pour the wine into the bottom of the cooker and place the chicken, breast side up, on the rack.

Cover and cook on HIGH for 30 minutes. Reduce the temperature setting to LOW and cook until the meat near the thighbone is very tender and the juices run clear when pierced with a fork, 7 to 7½ hours. Transfer the chicken to a carving board and reserve the pan juices. Remove the rack.

Pour the pan juices into a glass measuring cup and set it into the freezer for 5 minutes. Meanwhile, juice half of the orange. Set aside. Using a sharp knife, remove all skin and white pith from the second orange half. Remove the orange segments, discarding the membranes. Set the orange segments aside.

Take the measuring cup from the freezer and skim off and discard all fat that rose to the surface. Pour the skimmed pan juices back into the cooker and turn the temperature setting to HIGH. Add the orange juice, orange segments, and vinegar to the cooker. Cook on HIGH until the mixture thickens slightly and orange segments are heated through, about 10 minutes.

Carve the chicken and arrange on a heated large serving platter. Spoon the sauce over the chicken and serve.

○ PER SERVING: 4 g carbohydrate (includes 1 g dietary fiber), 39 g protein, 5 g fat, 229 calories
○ DIABETIC EXCHANGES: 5 lean meat

Stewed Chicken, Jamaican Style

MAKES 4 SERVINGS

1 large green bell pepper, cut
    into julienne strips
1 cup thinly sliced scallions,
    white part and 1 inch green
4 ounces button mushrooms,
    cleaned and thinly sliced
1 (4-ounce) can sliced
    pimientos, with liquid
½ teaspoon crushed dried
    oregano
1 (3-pound) whole roaster-fryer
    chicken, cut into 8 serving
    pieces
½ cup chopped fresh parsley
1 cup dry white wine
1 cup canned low-sodium
    chicken broth
Salt and freshly ground pepper,
    to taste
Bottle of Pickapeppa sauce
    (optional)

Years ago, my husband and I drove across the Jamaican Blue Mountains from the city of Kingston to the beach resort of Ocho Rios. About halfway, we stopped to visit a small church perched at the top of one of the mountains. A tiny eatery was housed next door, its handmade sign by the roadside announcing what the cook had made that day. We opted for a bowl of stewed chicken, which smelled marvelous and tasted even better with mugs of rich, Blue Mountain coffee.

Of course, no meal in Jamaica is complete without a liberal dousing of most everything on the plate with Pickapeppa, Jamaica's legendary sweet pepper sauce. Be careful: It's high in carbs and heat.

In a 3½–quart or larger slow-cooker, combine the bell pepper, scallions, mushrooms, pimientos, and oregano. Rinse the chicken and remove the skin and any visible fat. Arrange the chicken on top and sprinkle with the parsley. Pour the wine and broth into the slow cooker.

Cover and cook on LOW for 8 to 10 hours or on HIGH for 4 to 5 hours. Transfer the chicken and vegetables to individual serving bowls and keep warm. Pour the pan juices into a saucepan and skim off any surface fat. Boil until reduced to about 1 cup, about 5 minutes. Taste and adjust seasoning as needed. Ladle the mixture over the chicken and serve. If using, pass the Pickapeppa to sprinkle over each serving.

○ **PER SERVING:** 7 g carbohydrate (includes 2 g dietary fiber), 49 g protein, 12 g fat, 345 calories
○ **DIABETIC EXCHANGES:** 1½ vegetable, 6½ lean meat, ½ fat

Herb-Roasted Chicken

Years ago when I worked with Gayelord Hauser on the revision of his Mirror, Mirror on the Wall, *I was frequently invited to lunch after our twice-weekly meetings, especially when he was entertaining house-guests. At one such occasion he made a superb roasted chicken served on a bed of rocket (arugula) that he grew in his garden. His house-guest was the legendary film actress Greta Garbo. I never got the exact recipe, but the idea was simple—a stuffing of orange, onion, and fresh herbs with olive oil and dried herbs rubbed onto the skin. If you only have dried herbs, use one-third less than the amount of fresh herbs that are called for.*

Rinse the chicken; remove any visible fat. Pat the chicken dry with paper towels. Place the onions, oranges, garlic, and the fresh herbs in the cavity of the chicken. Place the chicken in a 5-quart or larger crockery slow cooker. Brush the chicken with the olive oil and sprinkle with the dried herbs. Season with salt and pepper.

Cover and cook on LOW for 6 to 7 hours or on HIGH for 3 to 3½ hours, until the meat near the thighbone is very tender and the juices run clear when pierced with a fork. Transfer the chicken to a carving board and let stand for 10 minutes. Drain the onion–orange juices from the cavity into a small bowl and cut the chicken into individual pieces.

Arrange the arugula on a large serving platter and top with the chicken pieces. Spoon the juices from the cavity into a serving dish to serve alongside the chicken.

○ PER SERVING: 13 g carbohydrate (includes 3 g dietary fiber), 41 g protein, 8 g fat, 287 calories

○ DIABETIC EXCHANGES: 1 vegetable, 5 lean meat, ½ fat

MAKES 6 SERVINGS

1 (4-pound) whole roaster-fryer chicken

2 medium onions, diced

2 medium navel oranges, peeled and diced

3 cloves garlic, minced

1 tablespoon fresh rosemary leaves

½ tablespoon minced fresh basil

½ tablespoon minced flat-leaf parsley

½ tablespoon minced fresh oregano

½ tablespoon minced fresh sage

½ tablespoon fresh thyme leaves

1 tablespoon extra-virgin olive oil

¼ teaspoon crushed dried basil

¼ teaspoon crushed dried oregano

¼ teaspoon crushed dried rosemary

¼ teaspoon crushed dried sage

¼ teaspoon crushed dried thyme

Salt and freshly ground pepper, to taste

2 bunches arugula, washed and crisped

Chicken, Havana Style

MAKES 6 SERVINGS

1 (4-pound) whole roaster-fryer
   chicken
½ cup dry white wine or water
½ cup fresh lime juice
2 tablespoons unsalted butter,
   melted
1 teaspoon ground cumin
1 teaspoon crushed dried
   oregano
¼ teaspoon garlic powder
⅛ teaspoon ground cloves

Last year my husband wanted our Thanksgiving turkey roasted Cuban style, a cooking method he'd been reading about on the Internet. The turkey was to be marinated in lime juice and spices for a day, and then roasted. I modified the technique and spice combination. The result was so delicious that I use the recipe for both turkey and chicken; here it's a done in a crockery slow cooker.

Rinse the chicken; remove any visible fat in the neck and body cavity. Place a wire rack or metal trivet in the bottom of a 5-quart or larger crockery slow cooker. Place the chicken, breast side up, on the rack. Pour the wine into the slow cooker. Combine the lime juice and butter; brush the mixture over the chicken. Combine the cumin, oregano, garlic powder, and cloves. Sprinkle over the chicken.

Cover and cook on LOW 7½ to 8 hours or on HIGH for 3½ to 4 hours, until the meat near the thighbone is very tender when pierced with a fork and the juices run clear.

If a browner, crisper skin is desired, carefully transfer the chicken to the rack of a broiler pan and broil 4 to 6 inches below the heat until golden brown, about 5 minutes. Transfer the chicken to a carving board and let rest for 10 minutes before carving into pieces, discarding the skin. If desired, strain the pan juices to pass separately.

○ **PER SERVING:** 2 g carbohydrate (includes trace dietary fiber), 39 g protein, 9 g fat, 250 calories
○ **DIABETIC EXCHANGES:** 5½ lean meat, ½ fat

Chicken with Lots of Garlic

Julia Child popularized this Provençal recipe for chicken roasted with 40 cloves of garlic on her successful 1970s cooking show. The garlic cloves mellow and sweeten as they cook in their skins, leaving a delicious, creamy, garlicky purée to squeeze onto the chicken. I like to roast the chicken on a bed of fresh fennel, but you could substitute celery if you like.

Place the fennel in the bottom of a 3½-quart or larger crockery slow cooker. Rinse the chicken; discard any visible fat. Pat the chicken dry with paper towels. Toss the chicken pieces with the olive oil. Arrange the chicken on top of the fennel. Season with salt and pepper; sprinkle with the tarragon and thyme. Scatter the garlic cloves around the chicken.

Cover and cook on LOW for 8 to 10 hours or on HIGH for 4 to 5 hours, until the meat near the thighbone is tender and the juices run clear when pierced. To serve, arrange the fennel, chicken, and garlic cloves on a heated serving platter.

○ **PER SERVING:** 9 g carbohydrate (includes 2 g dietary fiber), 40 g protein, 15 g fat, 336 calories
○ **DIABETIC EXCHANGES:** ½ vegetable, 5½ lean meat, 1 fat

MAKES 6 SERVINGS

1 large bulb fennel, trimmed, cored, and cut into julienne strips
1 (3½-pound) roaster-fryer chicken, cut into 6 serving pieces
2 tablespoons extra-virgin olive oil
Salt and freshly ground pepper, to taste
1 teaspoon crushed dried tarragon
½ teaspoon crushed dried thyme
4 heads garlic, cloves separated but not peeled

Chicken Cacciatore

MAKES 4 SERVINGS

1 (3-pound) roaster-fryer
   chicken, cut into quarters
Salt and freshly ground pepper,
   to taste
1 tablespoon extra-virgin olive
   oil
1 medium onion, finely minced
2 cloves garlic, finely minced
4 medium ribs celery with
   leaves, thinly sliced
2 teaspoons crushed dried
   rosemary
¼ teaspoon crushed red pepper
   flakes
1 (28-ounce) can crushed
   tomatoes
¼ cup marsala wine or canned
   low-sodium chicken broth

Most everyone loves chicken prepared in this fragrant combination of onion, garlic, rosemary, tomatoes, and one of Italy's national vegetables, celery. For best texture, brown the chicken pieces before they go into the slow cooker.

Rinse the chicken pieces and pat dry with paper towels. Season with salt and pepper. Heat the oil in a large nonstick skillet over medium-high heat. Add the chicken and sauté until golden brown, about 5 minutes per side, turning once.

Place the onion, garlic, and celery in the bottom of a 5-quart or larger crockery slow cooker. Arrange the chicken quarters on top and sprinkle with the rosemary and red pepper flakes. Pour the tomatoes and marsala over the chicken.

Cover and cook on LOW for 7 to 9 hours or on HIGH for 3½ to 4½ hours, until the chicken is very tender and the juices run clear when pierced with a fork. Transfer the chicken to warmed dinner plates, along with the pan sauce.

○ **PER SERVING:** 21 g carbohydrate (includes 6 g dietary fiber), 39 g protein, 9 g fat, 313 calories
○ **DIABETIC EXCHANGES:** 3½ vegetable, 5½ lean meat

Sonoma Chicken in a Pot

Sonoma is California wine country and this chicken dish embodies the vivid flavors of the region. Soft polenta (see page 62) would make a perfect foil for this bold-flavored dish. The garlic in the sauce is tamed significantly by blanching the cloves in boiling water before slow cooking.

Blanch the garlic cloves in boiling water to cover for 1 minute. Drain and refresh under cold water to stop the cooking. Drain again and place with the tomatoes in the bottom of a 5-quart or larger crockery slow cooker.

Rinse the chicken; discard any fat. Season with pepper and arrange on the tomatoes. Whisk together the wine, broth, and tomato paste. Pour over the chicken.

Cover and cook on LOW for 6 to 7 hours, or until the meat near the thighbone is very tender when pierced with a fork. Transfer the chicken to a plate and keep warm. Increase the temperature setting to HIGH, add the olives and capers, and cook, uncovered, until the pan sauce is reduced by half, 10 to 15 minutes. Return the chicken to the cooker and reheat the chicken thoroughly, occasionally spooning the sauce over the chicken, 5 to 10 minutes.

Transfer the chicken to a heated serving platter and drizzle the sauce over the top. Garnish with the parsley and serve at once.

○ PER SERVING: 7 g carbohydrate (includes 1 g dietary fiber), 53 g protein, 24 g fat, 474 calories
○ DIABETIC EXCHANGES: 1/2 vegetable, 7 1/2 lean meat

MAKES 6 SERVINGS

18 cloves garlic, peeled and each clove cut in half
2 cups peeled, seeded, chopped tomatoes (fresh or canned)
6 whole chicken legs with thighs attached (about 3 pounds total)
Freshly ground pepper, to taste
1 1/4 cups dry red wine, such as Cabernet Sauvignon, Chianti, or Shiraz
3/4 cup canned low-sodium chicken broth
2 tablespoons tomato paste
3/4 cup kalamata or Niçoise olives, pitted
2 tablespoons capers, rinsed and drained
2 tablespoons chopped fresh parsley

COOKING WITH ALCOHOL

Alcohol boils at a lower temperature than water, so much of the alcohol used in cooking is burned off, leaving only the flavor of wine, beer, or spirits used. This chart shows the percentage of alcohol remaining and is based on the most recent research by the U.S. Department of Agriculture.

COOKING METHOD	PERCENTAGE ALCOHOL REMAINING
Alcohol added to boiling liquid and removed from the heat	85
Flamed	75
Stirred in and banked or simmered for	
15 minutes	40
30 minutes	35
45 minutes	30
1 hour	25
1½ hours	20
2 hours	10
2½ hours	5

For ideas on what to substitute for alcohol in recipes, see page 120.

Chicken with an Intense Red Pepper Sauce

When I first sampled this chicken while cruising off the coast of Naples, I was taken by its beautiful presentation—a partially boned back quarter of a chicken covered by a shiny bright red sauce over a drift of creamy polenta made from white cornmeal. When I later visited the chef in the galley, he told me that the chicken had been slowly baked with the red bell peppers, the sauce reduced, and then puréed. The dish is easily adaptable to a slow cooker. If you're serving this for a special meal, ask your butcher to remove the thighbone, leaving the skin and drumstick attached.

Rinse the chicken; remove any fat. Pat the chicken dry with paper towels. Season with salt and pepper. Heat the oil in a large nonstick skillet over medium-high heat. Add the chicken and brown on each side for 5 minutes, turning once. Sprinkle with the rosemary, thyme, and red pepper flakes.

Place the bell peppers and garlic in the bottom of a 4-quart or larger crockery slow cooker. Arrange the chicken on top and add the tomatoes with juice and the wine.

Cover and cook on LOW for 7 to 9 hours or on HIGH for 3½ to 4½ hours. Transfer the chicken pieces to a heated serving platter and keep warm. Transfer the pan sauce to a food processor or blender; purée until smooth. If the mixture is too thin, transfer to a saucepan over medium-high heat. Boil, stirring, until reduced to desired consistency. Spoon the sauce over the chicken and serve immediately.

○ PER SERVING: 11 g carbohydrate (includes 1 g dietary fiber), 53 g protein, 25 g fat, 497 calories

○ DIABETIC EXCHANGES: 1½ vegetable, 7 lean meat

MAKES 4 SERVINGS

4 whole chicken legs with thighs attached

Salt and freshly ground pepper, to taste

1 tablespoon extra-virgin olive oil

1 teaspoon crushed dried rosemary

1 teaspoon crushed dried thyme

¼ teaspoon crushed red pepper flakes

2 large red bell peppers, thinly sliced

4 cloves garlic, thinly sliced

1 (14½-ounce) can whole plum tomatoes, including juice

½ cup dry red wine or canned low-sodium chicken broth

Roman Chicken

MAKES 6 SERVINGS

1 medium onion, thinly sliced

3 cloves garlic, minced

1 large red bell pepper, sliced

6 whole chicken legs with
thighs attached

1 (15-ounce) can tomato sauce

1 cup pitted black olives,
preferably kalamata

1 tablespoon capers, rinsed and
drained

¼ cup chopped fresh flat-leaf
parsley

Over the years, my friend Pat Eby has contributed several great recipes to my cookbooks. When this recipe arrived, I was glad that I had just purchased whole chicken legs on sale that morning and had an opened jar of kalamata olives in the fridge. In a matter of minutes, my dinner entrée for that night was simmering away in a slow cooker. Delicious!

Place the onion, garlic, and bell pepper in the bottom of a 4-quart or larger crockery slow cooker. Rinse the chicken pieces and pat dry with paper towels. Arrange on top of the vegetables and pour the tomato sauce over all.

Cover and cook on LOW for 7 to 8 hours or on HIGH for 3½ to 4 hours. Stir in the olives and capers during the last 30 minutes of cooking time. Arrange the chicken pieces on a heated serving platter and spoon the sauce over the chicken. Sprinkle with the parsley and serve immediately.

○ **PER SERVING:** 9 g carbohydrate (includes 2 g dietary fiber), 53 g protein, 24 g fat, 474 calories

○ **DIABETIC EXCHANGES:** 1½ vegetable, 7½ lean meat

Normandy-Style Chicken with Calvados and Apples

Normandy is the apple-growing region of France and home to this succulent chicken dish flamed with Calvados and enriched with heavy cream.

Rinse the chicken; remove any fat. Pat the chicken dry with paper towels. Season with salt and pepper. Heat the oil in a large nonstick skillet over medium-high heat. Add the chicken and sauté until nicely browned on both sides, turning once, about 10 minutes. Pour the Calvados over the chicken and, using a long wooden match, carefully ignite the Calvados. Spoon the pan juices over the chicken until the flames subside.

Place the onion and celery in the bottom of a 5-quart or larger crockery slow cooker. Transfer the chicken to the cooker and arrange the apple pieces on top. Stir the broth into the skillet and, using a wooden spoon, scrape the bottom to loosen any browned bits. Pour the mixture over the chicken.

Cover and cook on LOW for 6 to 8 hours or on HIGH for 3 to 4 hours. Transfer the chicken and apples to a heated serving platter and keep warm. If cooking on LOW, increase the temperature setting to HIGH. Whisk the dissolved cornstarch into the slow cooker and cook, stirring occasionally, until the mixture boils and thickens, about 10 minutes. Whisk in the heavy cream and thyme. Cook until heated through, but not boiling. Spoon the sauce over the chicken and apples. Serve immediately.

○ PER SERVING: 15 g carbohydrate (includes 3 g dietary fiber), 53 g protein, 31 g fat, 359 calories
○ DIABETIC EXCHANGES: 1/2 fruit, 1/2 vegetable, 71/2 lean meat, 1/2 fat

MAKES 4 SERVINGS

4 whole chicken legs with thighs attached
Salt and freshly ground pepper, to taste
1 tablespoon olive oil
1/3 cup Calvados
1/4 cup finely chopped onion
1/4 cup finely chopped celery
2 medium red apples, such as Gala, unpeeled, cored, and thinly sliced
1 cup canned low-sodium chicken broth
1 tablespoon cornstarch dissolved in 2 tablespoons water
1/4 cup heavy cream
1 teaspoon fresh thyme leaves

Roasted Chicken with Lemon and Olives

MAKES 4 SERVINGS

4 whole chicken legs with
    thighs attached
Salt and freshly ground pepper,
    to taste
1 tablespoon extra-virgin olive
    oil
1 medium onion, grated
2 cloves garlic, minced
1/2 teaspoon ground ginger
1/4 teaspoon ground cinnamon
Pinch cayenne pepper
Pinch saffron threads
1/2 cup canned low-sodium
    chicken broth
1 tablespoon grated lemon zest
1 cup green olives, rinsed
2 tablespoons chopped fresh
    cilantro, divided

If this were truly Moroccan, the recipe would call for a preserved lemon, which is hard to come by unless you preserve it yourself. Instead I've used a goodly amount of lemon zest along with customary green olives in the sauce and slow-roasted the chicken over a bed of onions and spices to simulate the flavors of exotic Morocco. I found some imported picholine olives at a local market, but domestic green olives are fine; just don't used olives stuffed with pimiento.

Rinse the chicken; discard any fat. Pat the chicken dry with paper towels. Season with salt and pepper. Heat the olive oil over medium-high heat in a large nonstick skillet. Add the chicken and sauté until chicken is nicely browned, about 5 minutes per side.

Toss the onion with the garlic, ginger, cinnamon, cayenne, and saffron. Place in the bottom of a 5-quart or larger crockery slow cooker. Arrange the chicken on top. Add the broth to the skillet and cook for 2 minutes, stirring with a wooden spoon to loosen any browned bits. Pour the mixture over the chicken.

Cover and cook on LOW for 6 to 7 hours or on HIGH for 3 to 3½ hours, until the juices run clear when the chicken is pierced with a knife near the thighbone. Transfer the chicken to a heated serving platter and keep warm. If cooking on LOW, increase the temperature setting to HIGH. Stir the lemon zest, olives, and 1 tablespoon of the cilantro into the pan juices. Cook for about 5 minutes, until the olives are heated through. Using a slotted spoon, remove the olives and arrange around the chicken pieces. Sprinkle with the remaining cilantro. Pour the pan juices into a gravy boat and pass separately to spoon over the chicken.

○ **PER SERVING:** 6 g carbohydrate (includes 1 g dietary fiber), 59 g protein, 28 g fat, 498 calories
○ **DIABETIC EXCHANGES:** ½ vegetable, 7½ lean meat

Slow-Cooked Chicken with Cabbage, Apples, and Bacon

This is a delightful way to prepare chicken and have your dinner virtually done in one pot. All that's needed is a salad of tossed greens, and you're finished.

Rinse the chicken; discard the skin and any lumps of fat. Pat the chicken dry with paper towels. Season with salt and pepper. Melt the butter in a nonstick skillet over medium-high heat. Add the chicken and sauté on both sides until nicely browned, about 10 minutes.

Meanwhile, place the cabbage in the bottom of a 5-quart or larger crockery slow cooker. Top with the onion and the apples. Lay the chicken pieces on top. In a measuring cup, combine the broth, wine, and thyme. Pour over the chicken.

Cover and cook on LOW for 6 to 7 hours or on HIGH for 3 to 3½ hours, until the juices near the thighbone run clear when pierced with a fork. Divide the vegetable mixture among 4 dinner plates and top each serving with a chicken piece. Sprinkle with the bacon and serve immediately.

○ PER SERVING: 21 g carbohydrate (includes 7 g dietary fiber), 56 g protein, 26 g fat, 546 calories
○ DIABETIC EXCHANGES: ½ fruit, 2 vegetable, 7½ lean meat

MAKES 4 SERVINGS

4 whole chicken legs with thighs attached
Salt and freshly ground pepper, to taste
1 tablespoon unsalted butter
4 cups coarsely chopped savoy cabbage
1 small onion, chopped
2 medium apples, such as Granny Smith, unpeeled, cored, and cut into eighths
½ cup canned low-sodium chicken broth
¼ cup dry white wine or additional stock
½ teaspoon crushed dried thyme
2 strips lean bacon, cooked crisp, drained, and crumbled

Persian Chicken and Eggplant

MAKES 10 SERVINGS

10 large chicken thighs (about 3¾ pounds total)

5 medium eggplants (about 5 pounds total)

¼ cup olive oil

2 large onions, coarsely chopped

1½ teaspoons ground turmeric

1 teaspoon crushed dried Italian herb seasoning

Garlic powder, to taste

Salt and freshly ground pepper, to taste

1 (28-ounce) whole tomatoes, including juice

Juice of 2 lemons

The last time my Persian friend Parvine visited here in Texas, she prepared this wonderful dish. She cooked it on top of the stove, but it needed her constant attention. Although the dish does require some precooking, once it's inside the slow cooker it simmers away unattended. You can grill the eggplant the night or days before and either refrigerate or freeze it until you're ready to start cooking.

Light a grill or preheat the broiler.

Rinse the chicken thighs; discard the skin and all visible fat. Pat the chicken dry with paper towels. Using a vegetable peeler, remove the peel from the eggplants. Slice the eggplants lengthwise into pieces about 4 inches long and 1 inch thick. Lay the slices on a work surface and, using 3 tablespoons of the olive oil, lightly brush both sides with the oil. Grill the eggplant, a few slices at a time, for about 3 minutes per side, forming well-defined grill marks. Or broil for 3 minutes per side, turning once. Transfer the grilled eggplant to a large baking sheet and continue until all eggplant slices are grilled.

In a large nonstick skillet, sauté the onions in the remaining 1 tablespoon of the oil until golden, but not browned. Stir in the turmeric and cook for 1 minute. Transfer the onions to the bottom of a 5-quart or larger crockery slow cooker. Add the chicken to the skillet and sauté until golden brown on both sides, 2 to 3 minutes per side. Arrange the chicken in one side of the slow cooker, stacking as necessary. Carefully place the grilled eggplant slices on the other side, making layers as necessary. Sprinkle with the Italian seasoning, garlic powder, salt, and pepper. Cut the tomatoes into quarters and arrange over the chicken and eggplant. Drizzle with the juice from the tomatoes and the lemon juice.

Cover and cook on LOW for 7 to 8 hours or on HIGH for 3½ to 4 hours. Transfer the chicken to a heated, large serving dish. Carefully transfer the eggplant slices to the dish, lifting each slice carefully with a wide spatula to avoid breaking the slices. Spoon the tomatoes and onions over the top. Serve immediately.

○ **PER SERVING:** 23 g carbohydrate (includes 8 g dietary fiber), 23 g protein, 6 g fat, 224 calories
○ **DIABETIC EXCHANGES:** 4½ vegetable, 2½ lean meat

Chicken Thighs with Chiles and Cherries

MAKES 6 SERVINGS

1 medium onion, thinly sliced
  and separated into rings

2 cloves garlic, minced

1 to 2 jalapeño chiles, or to
  taste, seeded and minced

³/₄ cup coarsely chopped dried
  tart cherries

1 cup dry red wine

¹/₃ cup fresh orange juice

2 teaspoons grated orange zest

1 teaspoon sweet paprika

¹/₂ teaspoon crushed dried
  thyme

¹/₄ teaspoon cayenne pepper

6 (5-ounce) boneless, skinless
  chicken thighs

Salt and freshly ground pepper,
  to taste

Jalapeño chiles and dried tart cherries make a lively sauce for these chicken thighs. The dish is assembled in minutes, then cooks unattended for most of the day while you're away at work or play. If your local supermarket doesn't carry dried cherries, look for them at a natural foods store or buy them from the Internet. They'll keep in the refrigerator for months.

Place the onion, garlic, chiles, and cherries in the bottom of a 4-quart or larger crockery slow cooker. In a large measuring cup, combine the wine, orange juice, orange zest, paprika, thyme, and cayenne. Pour into the slow cooker.

Rinse the chicken; discard any fat. Pat the chicken dry with paper towels. Season with salt and pepper. Place the chicken in the slow cooker.

Cover and cook on LOW for 5 to 6 hours or on HIGH for 2½ to 3 hours, until the chicken is cooked through. Transfer the chicken to a heated serving platter. If cooking on LOW, increase the cooking temperature to HIGH. Stir the cooking liquids and cook, uncovered, for 5 to 10 minutes, until thickened slightly to make a sauce. Ladle the sauce over the chicken and serve.

○ **PER SERVING:** 17 g carbohydrate (includes 1 g dietary fiber), 38 g protein, 16 g fat, 370 calories

○ **DIABETIC EXCHANGES:** 1 fruit, ¹/₂ vegetable, 5 lean meat

Easy Paprika Chicken

This crockery version of Hungary's most famous chicken dish has all the flavor of the traditional dish but eliminates the need for constant attention. For the best flavor, make sure your paprika is Hungarian and fresh.

Rinse the chicken; remove the skin and any fat. Pat dry with paper towels. Season the chicken with salt and pepper. Heat the oil in a large nonstick skillet over medium-high heat. Add the chicken and sauté for 5 minutes per side, turning once. Transfer the chicken to the bottom of a 3½-quart or larger crockery slow cooker. Add the onion to the skillet and sauté until the onion is limp, about 4 minutes. Spoon the onion over the chicken. Add the mushrooms to the skillet and sauté, stirring, for 2 minutes. Spoon the mushrooms into the cooker. In a large measuring cup, combine the tomato soup, water, and wine. Pour over the chicken. Sprinkle with the paprika.

Cover and cook on LOW for 6 to 7 hours or on HIGH for 3 to 3½ hours. Transfer the chicken to a large, heated serving platter. If cooking on LOW, increase the cooking temperature to HIGH. In a medium bowl, whisk together the sour cream and flour. Stir ½ cup of the hot cooking liquid into the sour cream mixture. Add to the cooker, stirring to combine. Cook, uncovered, until thickened and bubbly, about 5 minutes. Pour the pan sauce over the chicken and serve.

○ PER SERVING: 5 g carbohydrate (includes 1 g dietary fiber), 38 g protein, 22 g fat, 380 calories
○ DIABETIC EXCHANGES: ½ vegetable, 5 lean meat

MAKES 6 SERVINGS

2½ pounds chicken thighs
Salt and freshly ground pepper, to taste
1 tablespoon extra-virgin olive oil
1 medium onion, minced
1 (6-ounce) package sliced mushrooms
1 (10¾-ounce) can condensed tomato soup
½ cup water
½ cup dry white wine or additional water
2 tablespoons Hungarian paprika
½ cup sour cream
1 tablespoon unbleached all-purpose flour

Creole Chicken Fricassee

MAKES 6 SERVINGS

3 pounds chicken pieces
Salt and freshly ground pepper,
    to taste
1 tablespoon extra-virgin olive
    oil
2 medium onions, chopped
2 medium red bell peppers, cut
    into 1-inch pieces
½ cup chopped celery
½ cup diced carrots
½ cup diced lean ham
2 cloves garlic, minced
1 (14½-ounce) can diced
    tomatoes, including juice
½ cup dry white wine or
    canned low-sodium chicken
    broth
2 bay leaves
1 teaspoon crushed dried thyme
1 teaspoon crushed dried
    oregano
2 tablespoons chopped fresh
    parsley

Using the typical trio of bell peppers, onions, and celery as its flavor base, this Creole chicken recipe has French roots but departs from a classic French chicken fricassee recipe with the omission of heavy cream.

Rinse the chicken; remove the skin and any fat. Pat dry with paper towels. Season the chicken with salt and pepper. In a large nonstick skillet, heat the olive oil over high heat. Add the chicken pieces and sauté until nicely browned, turning occasionally, about 10 minutes.

Meanwhile, layer the onions, bell peppers, celery, carrots, ham, and garlic in the bottom of a 5-quart or larger crockery slow cooker. Transfer the chicken pieces to the slow cooker. In a large measuring cup, combine the tomatoes with their juice, wine, bay leaves, thyme, and oregano. Pour over the chicken and vegetables.

Cover and cook on LOW for 6 to 8 hours or on HIGH for 3 to 4 hours, until the chicken is cooked through and the vegetables are tender. Transfer the chicken and vegetables to a heated serving platter. Discard the bay leaves. Sprinkle with the parsley and serve immediately.

O PER SERVING: 12 g carbohydrate (includes 2 g dietary fiber), 39 g protein, 12 g fat, 315 calories
O DIABETIC EXCHANGES: 2 vegetable, 5½ lean meat

African Chicken in Peanut Sauce with Crispy Leeks

The cook at my university sorority house was from the Congo and a source of a wealth of recipes that I enjoyed then and now. This spicy chicken was one of my favorites. The recipe has evolved some over the years, but not that much. You can use the crispy leeks to garnish any number of dishes.

Rinse the chicken; discard any lumps of fat. Pat dry with paper towels. Season the chicken with salt and pepper. Heat 1 tablespoon oil in a large nonstick skillet over medium-high heat. Add the chicken and brown, about 2 minutes per side. Remove from the heat and set aside.

Place the onion and garlic in the bottom of a 4-quart or larger crockery slow cooker. Stir in the tomato sauce, curry powder, and pepper flakes. Arrange the chicken pieces on top.

Cover and cook on LOW for 5 to 6 hours, until the juices near the thighbone run clear when pierced with the tip of a sharp knife. (Do not cook on HIGH or the sauce will curdle.) Transfer the chicken to a platter and keep warm. Whisk the peanut butter and yogurt into the pan juices. Return the chicken to the cooker and baste with the sauce. Let heat through for 5 minutes.

Meanwhile, bring a pot of water to a boil, add the leeks, and boil for 1 minute. While the leeks are boiling, heat ¼ inch of oil in a deep sauté pan to 350°F. Drain the leeks and pat dry with paper towels. Fry the leeks in the oil until crispy, 1 to 2 minutes. Remove from the pan and drain on paper towels.

To serve, transfer the chicken pieces to a heated serving platter. Taste the sauce and add cayenne pepper, if desired. Spoon the sauce over the chicken and top with the leeks. Serve immediately.

MAKES 6 SERVINGS

6 (6-ounce) boneless, skinless chicken thighs
Salt and freshly ground pepper, to taste
1 tablespoon canola oil plus extra for frying leeks
1 medium onion, chopped
3 cloves garlic, minced
1 (8-ounce) can tomato sauce
1 teaspoon curry powder
½ teaspoon crushed red pepper flakes
½ cup natural-style peanut butter
½ cup plain low-fat yogurt
2 leeks, white part and pale green, rinsed well and julienned
Cayenne pepper, to taste (optional)

○ **PER SERVING:** 13 g carbohydrate (includes 3 g dietary fiber), 40 g protein, 26 g fat, 396 calories
○ **DIABETIC EXCHANGES:** 1½ vegetable, 6 lean meat

Slow-Cooked Chicken Casserole

MAKES 8 SERVINGS

8 (6-ounce) boneless, skinless
  chicken thighs
16 dried apricot halves
8 dried pitted prunes
6 ounces button mushrooms,
  sliced
2 medium onions, thinly sliced
1 medium navel orange
2 large lemons
½ tablespoon crushed dried
  thyme
Salt and freshly ground pepper,
  to taste
2 tablespoons extra-virgin olive
  oil

*Great for a family gathering, this special chicken dish is full of flavor
and liked by both adults and children.*

Rinse the chicken; discard any lumps of fat. Pat dry with paper
towels. Arrange the chicken in the bottom of a 5-quart or
larger crockery slow cooker. Scatter the apricots, prunes, and
mushrooms around the chicken. Cover with the onions. Thinly
slice the orange and lemons (do not peel). Remove any seeds.
Arrange the fruit slices on top of the onions. Scatter the thyme
over all. Season with salt and pepper. Drizzle with the olive oil.

Cover and cook on LOW for 8 to 10 hours or on HIGH
for 4 to 5 hours, until the chicken is done and the juices run
clear when pierced near the thighbone. To serve, arrange the
chicken and fruit on a heated serving platter. Arrange vegetables
over and around. Serve at once.

○ **PER SERVING:** 22 g carbohydrate (includes 4 g dietary fiber), 46 g
  protein, 22g fat, 470 calories
○ **DIABETIC EXCHANGES:** 1 fruit, 1 vegetable, 6 lean meat, ½ fat

Creamy Chicken Dijon

This chicken dish is full of the flavors one experiences in Dijon, France—the home of the spicy mustard of the same name and the capital of Burgundy. Because most families are split in their preferences for white and dark meat, I've used both in the recipe. You can, of course, use all white or all dark with no difference in the carb count.

Cut the trimmed leeks in half lengthwise and wash well. Thinly slice on the diagonal. Place the leeks in the bottom of a 5-quart or larger crockery slow cooker.

Rinse the chicken; discard any fat. Pat dry with paper towels. Season with salt and pepper. In a small dish, combine the Dijon mustard and tarragon. Spread on the chicken pieces and wrap strips of the prosciutto around each piece. Place the chicken on top of the leeks. Pour the wine over the chicken.

Cover and cook on LOW for 5 to 6 hours or on HIGH for 2½ to 3 hours. Transfer the chicken to a heated serving platter. If cooking on LOW, increase the temperature setting to HIGH. Whisk the cream into the pan juices and cook, uncovered, until sauce is slightly thickened, about 5 minutes. Spoon the sauce over the chicken. Serve immediately.

○ **PER SERVING:** 5 g carbohydrate (includes trace dietary fiber), 24 g protein, 12 g fat, 222 calories

○ **DIABETIC EXCHANGES:** ½ vegetable, 3 lean meat, 1 fat

MAKES 6 SERVINGS

2 large leeks, white part and 1 inch pale green

3 boneless, skinless chicken breast halves

3 boneless, skinless chicken thighs

Salt and freshly ground pepper, to taste

2 tablespoons Dijon mustard

½ teaspoon crushed dried tarragon

1½ ounces prosciutto, cut into 1-inch wide strips

½ cup white Burgundy wine or low-sodium canned chicken broth

½ cup heavy cream

Chicken Veracruz

MAKES 6 SERVINGS

6 boneless, skinless chicken
    breast halves (about 2
    pounds total)
18 to 24 slices pickled jalapeño
    chiles
1 tablespoon minced garlic
1 tablespoon fresh lime juice
1½ teaspoons crushed dried
    oregano, preferably Mexican
3 tablespoons chopped fresh
    flat-leaf parsley
1 medium onion, thinly sliced
1 (28-ounce) can whole
    tomatoes, including juice
1 cup pitted green olives, sliced,
    divided
2 tablespoons capers, rinsed
    and drained, divided
¼ cup dry red wine
2 tablespoons tomato paste

The same seasonings that go into red snapper Veracruz—tomatoes, capers, olives, and herbs—can be used to make a fabulous chicken dish. For my taste, I've stuffed the pounded chicken breast halves with slices of pickled jalapeño chiles, but if you prefer a milder flavor, use minced green bell pepper. You can buy jars of pickled jalapeño chiles in the Mexican aisle of most well-stocked supermarkets or a Mexican grocery store.

Rinse the chicken; discard any fat. Pat dry with paper towels. Place each breast between 2 sheets of plastic wrap and lightly pound with a mallet to flatten evenly to about ½-inch thickness. Place 3 or 4 pickled jalapeño slices and ½ teaspoon of the minced garlic in the center of each chicken piece. Fold in the sides, enclosing the chiles and garlic. Drizzle the lime juice onto the chicken. In a small dish, combine the oregano and parsley. Sprinkle the mixture over the filled chicken breasts. Set aside.

Place the onion in the bottom of a 3½-quart crockery slow cooker. Drain the tomatoes, reserving the juice. Thickly slice the tomatoes and place on top of the onion. Sprinkle with half of the olives and half of the capers. Place the chicken breasts on top of the tomatoes. Combine the reserved tomato juice, wine, and tomato paste. Pour over the chicken.

Cover and cook on LOW for 5 to 6 hours or on HIGH for 2½ to 3 hours. To serve, transfer the chicken breasts to a heated serving platter. Spoon the cooking sauce over the chicken and sprinkle with the remaining olives and capers. Serve immediately.

○ **PER SERVING:** 11 g carbohydrate (includes 2 g dietary fiber), 37 g protein, 6 g fat. 235 calories
○ **DIABETIC EXCHANGES:** 2 vegetable, 5 lean meat

Easy Asian Chicken

If you like the flavors of southeast Asia—sweet-sour, salty, and hot— you're sure to love this easy chicken dish. Serve the chicken on a bed of shredded red cabbage for a complete meal and offer everyone a tangerine or clementine for dessert.

Place the bell pepper, onion, garlic, and water chestnuts in the bottom of a 3½-quart or larger crockery slow cooker.

Rinse the chicken; discard any fat. Pat dry with paper towels. Arrange the chicken on top of the vegetables and add the zest. In a large measuring cup, combine the remaining ingredients *except* the cabbage and cashews. Pour over the chicken.

Cover and cook on LOW for 5 to 7 hours or on HIGH for 2½ to 3½ hours, until the chicken is cooked through. Pile the cabbage on a large serving platter and top with the chicken, vegetables, and pan sauce. Sprinkle with the cashews and serve immediately.

○ PER SERVING: 19 g carbohydrate (includes 4 g dietary fiber), 37 g protein, 6 g fat, 274 calories

○ DIABETIC EXCHANGES: 2 vegetable, 5 lean meat

MAKES 6 SERVINGS

1 large red bell pepper, thinly sliced
1 cup chopped onion
2 cloves garlic, minced
1 (8-ounce) can sliced water chestnuts, drained
6 (5-ounce) boneless, skinless chicken thighs
4 (2-inch) strips orange zest
½ cup reduced-sodium soy sauce
1 tablespoon light brown sugar
1 tablespoon balsamic vinegar
1 tablespoon hoisin sauce
1 tablespoon grated fresh ginger
2 teaspoons Thai red curry paste
3 cups shredded red cabbage
⅓ cup roasted cashews

Chicken with Cream Gravy

MAKES 4 SERVINGS

4 (5-ounce) boneless, skinless chicken breast halves

1 clove garlic, minced

1 (10¾-ounce) can condensed cream of chicken soup

1 cup white wine

1 tablespoon Worcestershire sauce

1 (8-ounce) package cream cheese, cut into small pieces

Snipped fresh chives for garnish (optional)

Such an easy dish to have such wonderful flavor, this works well with boneless, skinless chicken thighs if you prefer dark meat.

Rinse the chicken; discard any fat. Pat dry with paper towels. Arrange the chicken in the bottom of a 3½-quart or larger crockery slow cooker. Sprinkle with the garlic. In a large measuring cup, combine the soup, wine, and Worcestershire sauce. Pour over the chicken.

Cover and cook on LOW for 5 to 6 hours or on HIGH for 2½ to 3 hours. During the last 30 minutes of cooking time, stir in the cream cheese. When ready to serve, transfer the chicken to individual serving plates. Whisk the sauce in the cooker to make a smooth gravy. Ladle some of the sauce over each serving and, if using, garnish with chives. Serve immediately.

O **PER SERVING:** 9 g carbohydrate (includes trace dietary fiber), 39 g protein, 26 g fat, 438 calories

O **DIABETIC EXCHANGES:** ½ bread/starch, 5½ lean meat, 2 fat

Pizza Chicken

*My sister Eileen came up with this easy recipe for her young grand-
daughters, who'd rather eat pizza than most anything. They loved it,
as did the adults.*

Rinse the chicken; discard any fat. Pat dry with paper towels.
Place the Parmesan cheese on a large plate and mix in the Italian seasoning. Dip each chicken piece in the egg mixture and
then in the cheese mixture, turning to coat all sides. Set aside
until all pieces are coated.

Heat the olive oil in a large nonstick skillet. Add the
chicken pieces and sauté until golden brown on both sides,
about 8 minutes. Transfer the chicken to a 3½-quart or larger
crockery slow cooker. Cover the chicken with the pizza sauce
and sprinkle with the pepperoni.

Cover and cook on LOW for 5 to 6 hours or on HIGH for
2½ to 3 hours. Sprinkle the cheese on top and continue to
cook, covered, for 5 to 10 minutes, until the cheese melts. Transfer the chicken and sauce to a serving dish and serve hot.

○ PER SERVING: 18 g carbohydrate (includes 4 g dietary fiber), 41 g protein, 20 g fat, 428 calories
○ DIABETIC EXCHANGES: 3 vegetable, 5½ lean meat, 1 fat

MAKES 6 SERVINGS

1½ pounds boneless, skinless
   chicken breast halves
1 cup freshly grated Parmesan
   cheese
½ teaspoon crushed dried
   Italian herb seasoning
2 large eggs, beaten with 1
   tablespoon water
2 tablespoons olive oil
1 (28-ounce) jar meatless pizza
   or pasta sauce
½ cup chopped pepperoni
½ cup shredded mozzarella
   cheese

Sicilian Chicken with Vegetables

MAKES 6 SERVINGS

1 medium onion, chopped

2 cloves garlic, minced

1 (8-ounce) package frozen
   artichoke hearts

12 ounces sliced portobello
   mushrooms, cleaned

6 boneless, skinless chicken
   breast halves (about 2
   pounds total)

1 cup canned low-sodium
   chicken broth

¼ cup dry white wine

3 tablespoons fresh lemon juice

½ teaspoon crushed dried basil

6 thin slices prosciutto,
   chopped

¼ cup chopped fresh flat-leaf
   parsley

1 tablespoon grated lemon zest

Most markets carry sliced portobello mushrooms, which saves a little time in assembling this delicious dish. The minced prosciutto adds a nice finish, making this as perfect for company as it is for family. If your market doesn't carry prosciutto, you could use lean ham.

Place the onion and garlic in the bottom of a 4-quart or larger crockery slow cooker. Top with the artichoke hearts, mushrooms, and chicken. Combine the broth, wine, lemon juice, and basil. Pour over the chicken.

Cover and cook on LOW for 7 to 8 hours or on HIGH for 3½ to 4 hours, until the chicken and vegetables are tender. Transfer the chicken, vegetables, and pan sauce to a heated serving platter. Sprinkle with the prosciutto, parsley, and lemon zest. Serve immediately.

○ PER SERVING: 10 g carbohydrate (includes 4 g dietary fiber), 41 g protein, 14 g fat, 241 calories

○ DIABETIC EXCHANGES: 1½ vegetable, 5½ lean meat

CITRUS ZEST

In my cooking, I use a lot of citrus zest. When used in the small amounts indicated in the recipes and spread over the number of servings, it adds only a trace of carbohydrate. Zest adds amazing flavor to everything from soups to desserts.

You can buy a zester, including the new Microplane model, in gourmet cookware shops and many supermarkets, which makes it easy to remove the zest from the bitter white pith underneath. You can also use a handheld grater to remove the zest, but be careful not to nick your knuckles. If the grater is first wrapped with plastic wrap, the zest is easier to remove and it saves your knuckles a bit. Once the zest is removed, mince it finely unless otherwise directed by the recipe.

Anytime a large amount of zest (in excess of ¼ cup) is called for in a recipe, you can use the equivalent in drops of citrus oil to save a carb or two. These oils come in lemon, lime, and orange flavors and are available by mail order or over the Internet from Williams-Sonoma or King Arthur Flour.

Teriyaki Game Hens

Most everyone loves the taste of teriyaki sauce. Here you make the sauce from scratch while Cornish game hens slowly cook to tender perfection. Serve these hens with a stir-fry of Asian vegetables and your dinner's made—almost effortlessly! Ask your butcher to cut the hens in half; most will do so gladly, without charge.

MAKES 4 SERVINGS

2 (1¼-pound) Cornish game
  hens, cut in half lengthwise
Freshly ground pepper
2 tablespoons reduced-sodium
  soy sauce
1 tablespoon grated fresh
  ginger
1 clove garlic, minced
1 tablespoon dark brown sugar
½ teaspoon ground ginger
2 tablespoons dry sherry
1 tablespoon canola oil

Rinse the hens and pat dry. Lightly sprinkle with pepper. Place the hens, skin side down, in a 5-quart or larger crockery slow cooker. Combine the soy sauce, fresh ginger, garlic, brown sugar, ground ginger, sherry, and canola oil. Pour over the hens. Turn each hen over twice, ending with the skin side up, to evenly coat with the sauce.

Cover and cook on LOW for 10 to 11 hours or on HIGH for 5 to 5½ hours, until the hens are tender. To serve, transfer the hens to a heated serving platter. Skim and discard any surface fat from the pan sauce. Nap the hens with the remaining sauce.

O **PER SERVING:** 5 g carbohydrate (includes trace dietary fiber), 35 g protein, 9 g total fat, 250 calories
O **DIABETIC EXCHANGES:** 6 lean meat

Game Hens with Tomatoes and Tarragon Vinegar

MAKES 4 SERVINGS

5 shallots, minced

2 cloves garlic, minced

1¹/₂ pounds ripe tomatoes, seeded and coarsely chopped

4 (1¹/₄-pound) Cornish game hens

Salt and freshly ground pepper, to taste

1 tablespoon extra-virgin olive oil

¹/₂ cup low-sodium canned chicken broth

¹/₂ cup tarragon vinegar

2 tablespoons tomato paste

¹/₂ cup crème fraîche (see page 109) or heavy cream

2 tablespoons chopped fresh tarragon

The classic French combination of tomatoes and tarragon vinegar works as wonderfully with game hens as it does with chicken. If you're using a 5-quart or larger slow cooker, you can prepare the full recipe— using a 3¹/₂- or 4-quart cooker, you can only prepare half of the recipe, or you can use two cookers.

In the bottom of a 5-quart or larger crockery slow cooker, combine the shallots, garlic, and tomatoes.

Rinse the game hens; discard the giblets, necks, and any visible fat. Pat dry with paper towels. Season inside and out with salt and pepper. Tie the legs together with kitchen string. Heat the oil in a large nonstick skillet over medium-high heat. Add the hens and brown on all sides, about 10 minutes.

Transfer the hens to the cooker, placing them on their ends, neck side down. Add the broth, vinegar, and tomato paste to the skillet. Cook over medium heat for 3 to 4 minutes, scraping the bottom of the skillet with a wooden spoon to loosen any browned bits. Pour the mixture over the hens.

Cover and cook on LOW for 7 to 9 hours or on HIGH for 3½ to 4½ hours, until the hens are tender. Transfer the hens to a heated serving platter. Remove the strings and keep the hens warm.

If cooking on LOW, increase the temperature setting to HIGH. Cook, uncovered, until the pan sauce is thickened and reduced by roughly one-third, about 15 minutes. Stir in the crème fraîche. Continue to cook, stirring occasionally, for 5 minutes. Pour the sauce over the hens and sprinkle with the tarragon. Serve immediately.

○ **PER SERVING:** 5 g carbohydrate (includes trace dietary fiber), 70 g protein, 26 g fat, 550 calories

○ **DIABETIC EXCHANGES:** 1 vegetable, 10 lean meat, 1 fat

Crème Fraîche

Although several dairy producers now sell this slightly fermented cream in supermarkets, it's so easy and less expensive to make it at home. Crème fraîche is a marvelous addition to recipes, or you can use it as a topping for soups and desserts. It continues to thicken in the refrigerator and will keep for up to one week.

MAKES 2 CUPS

1 cup heavy cream
1 cup sour cream

Mix the two creams together and place in a large jar with a tight-fitting lid. Let set in a warm place for 12 hours, until the mixture thickens. Refrigerate until ready to use.

○ **PER 2-TABLESPOON SERVING:** 1 g carbohydrate (includes 0 dietary fiber), 1 g protein, 9 g fat, 82 calories
○ **DIABETIC EXCHANGES:** 1¹/₂ fat

Apricot Roasted Game Hens with Vegetables

MAKES 2 SERVINGS

1 cup whole baby carrots

¼ cup sliced shallots

2 (1¼-pound) Cornish game
  hens

Salt and freshly ground pepper,
  to taste

1 tablespoon extra-virgin olive
  oil

1 small Sweet Dumpling or
  acorn squash, seeded and
  cut into 4 wedges

¼ cup sugar-free apricot
  preserves

2 tablespoons warm water

¼ cup dry white wine or
  canned low-sodium chicken
  broth

1 teaspoon crushed dried thyme

You can buy sugar-free apricot preserves at most grocery stores to use in this delightful roasted game hen dinner.

Place the carrots and shallots in the bottom of a 3½-quart or larger crockery slow cooker.

Rinse the game hens; discard the giblets, necks, and any visible fat. Pat dry with paper towels. Season inside and out with salt and pepper. Tie the legs together with kitchen string. Heat the oil in a large nonstick skillet over medium-high heat. Add the hens and brown on all sides, about 10 minutes.

Transfer the hens to the cooker, placing them side by side. Place the squash wedges around the hens. Combine the apricot preserves and warm water. Using a pastry brush, first brush the insides of the squash and then the game hens with the apricot mixture. Add the wine to the cooker. Sprinkle with the thyme.

Cover and cook on LOW for 7 to 9 hours or on HIGH for 3½ to 4½ hours, until the hens and vegetables are tender. Transfer the hens to a heated serving platter. Remove the strings and keep the hens warm. Arrange the game hens and vegetables on a heated serving dish. Pour the pan juices over the hens and vegetables and serve.

○ PER SERVING: 25 g carbohydrate (includes 2 g dietary fiber), 70 g protein, 18 g fat, 552 calories

○ DIABETIC EXCHANGES: 3 vegetable, 10 lean meat, ½ fat

Roasted Turkey Breast Stuffed with Herbs, Prosciutto, and Cheese

A stuffed boneless turkey breast is perfect for a grand holiday dinner or anytime family gathering. Here I've stuffed the turkey breast with Parmesan cheese prosciutto and a mixture of parsley and thyme. It roasts to perfection on a bed of leeks and apples, which flavor the pan juices for the gravy.

MAKES 12 SERVINGS

- 1 (4-pound) boneless turkey breast with skin
- ½ cup chopped fresh flat-leaf parsley
- 2 tablespoons fresh thyme leaves
- ⅓ cup freshly grated Parmesan cheese
- 2 ounces prosciutto or lean ham, minced
- 4 medium leeks, white part and 2 inches green, well rinsed and thinly sliced on the diagonal
- 2 medium Granny Smith apples, peeled, cored, and chopped
- ½ cup dry white wine or water
- 1 (14-ounce) can low-sodium chicken broth
- 2 tablespoons Calvados or apple brandy (optional)
- 2 tablespoons unsalted butter, softened
- 2 tablespoons all-purpose flour

Rinse the turkey breast; pat dry with paper towels. With a flat mallet, gently pound the breast and, using your fingers, gently separate the turkey skin from the meat. Combine the parsley and thyme. Rub the turkey breast inside and out with the parsley mixture. Sprinkle the Parmesan and prosciutto over the inside to within 1½ inches of the edges. Roll the turkey lengthwise to form a log; replace the skin. Tie at 2-inch intervals with kitchen string.

Place the leeks and apples in the bottom of a 5-quart or larger crockery slow cooker. Top with the turkey breast, skin side up. Pour the wine over the turkey.

Cover and cook on LOW for 8 to 10 hours or on HIGH for 4 to 5 hours, until the turkey is tender. Transfer the turkey to a carving board and keep warm. Let stand for 10 minutes before carving into ½-inch slices.

Meanwhile, if cooking on LOW, increase the temperature setting to HIGH. Whisk the broth and Calvados, if using, into the pan drippings in the slow cooker. In a small bowl, combine the butter and flour. Whisk the flour mixture into the slow cooker and cook, uncovered, stirring occasionally, until the gravy is thickened and bubbly, about 15 minutes. Cook, stirring, for 1 minute. Pour the gravy into a gravy boat to spoon over the turkey slices. Arrange the turkey slices on a serving platter and serve.

○ PER 5-OUNCE SERVING: 8 g carbohydrate (includes 1 g dietary fiber), 40 g protein, 4 g fat, 242 calories

○ DIABETIC EXCHANGES: ½ fruit, ½ vegetable, 5 very lean meat

Turkey Tonnato with Arugula and Orange Slices

MAKES 12 SERVINGS

1 cup dry white wine

½ cup water

1 small onion, chopped

1 small carrot, chopped

1 rib celery, chopped

1 clove garlic, minced

1 (3-pound) boneless, skinless
   turkey breast, rolled and
   tied

Salt and freshly ground pepper,
   to taste

1 (6½-ounce) can water-packed
   white tuna, drained

2 tablespoons fresh lemon juice

4 anchovy fillets, rinsed and
   drained

¾ cup extra-virgin olive oil

4 large bunches arugula,
   washed and crisped

2 large navel oranges, peeled
   with all white pith removed,
   halved, and thinly sliced

1 tablespoon capers, rinsed and
   drained

An elegant dish for summer dinner party buffets, this can be made up to 2 days ahead and the ingredients won't wither in the heat. Traditionally this dish would be made with veal, but the use of turkey lightens the dish, and the mild turkey flavor is a perfect foil for the savory tuna sauce. The sweetness of the orange slices and the bite of the arugula further complement the dish. If you can't get arugula, substitute watercress.

In a 4-quart or larger crockery slow cooker, combine the wine, water, onion, carrot, celery, and garlic. Place the turkey breast in the cooker and season with salt and pepper.

Cover and cook on LOW for 5 to 6 hours, until an instant-read thermometer inserted in the center of the turkey breast registers 168°F. Uncover and let the turkey breast cool completely in the liquid, then discard the liquid.

In a food processor or blender, combine the tuna, lemon juice, and anchovies. With the machine running, gradually add the olive oil and process until smooth.

Remove the strings from the turkey breast and cut into ½-inch slices. Arrange the slices, overlapping, on a large serving tray. Spread the tuna mixture evenly over the turkey slices. Cover with plastic wrap and chill for at least 4 hours or overnight.

Just before serving, surround the edges of the platter with the arugula and tuck the orange slices between the arugula and the tonnato. Sprinkle the tonnato with the capers and serve.

○ **PER 4-OUNCE SERVING:** 5 g carbohydrate (includes 1 g dietary fiber), 33 g protein, 16 g fat, 220 calories

○ **DIABETIC EXCHANGES:** ½ fruit, 4 very lean meat, 2½ fat

Turkey Meatballs Alfredo

When you're setting up your slow cooker before you rush off to work and you're running late, you don't want to fuss with a lot of ingredients. All of the main ingredients in this recipe may be purchased from the store ready to cook, so this is a busy-day keeper. No need to thaw the meatballs ahead of time, they'll cook fine in the sauce from the frozen state.

MAKES 4 SERVINGS

2 (12-ounce) packages frozen Italian-style turkey meatballs

1 (16-ounce) jar Alfredo pasta sauce

1/2 teaspoon crushed dried Italian herb seasoning

2 cups hot cooked whole wheat noodles (optional)

1/4 cup finely shredded Parmesan cheese

2 tablespoons chopped fresh basil

Place the meatballs in the bottom of a 3½-quart or larger crockery slow cooker. Combine the pasta sauce and Italian seasoning. Spoon over the meatballs.

Cover and cook on LOW for 8 to 9 hours or on HIGH for 4 to 4½ hours. Place the hot cooked noodles on each of 4 serving plates, if using. Top with the meatballs and sauce. Sprinkle with the Parmesan cheese and basil. Serve immediately.

○ PER SERVING (MEATBALLS AND SAUCE ONLY): 7 g carbohydrate (includes 1 g dietary fiber), 39 g protein, 29 g fat, 445 calories

○ DIABETIC EXCHANGES: 1/2 bread/starch, 5½ lean meat, 2½ fat

Barbecued Turkey Thighs

MAKES 6 SERVINGS

2 cups Aunt Miriam's Barbecue
   Sauce (page 129), divided
2 boneless, skinless turkey
   thighs (about 2½ pounds
   total)
1 small red onion, quartered
   and thinly sliced
¼ teaspoon crushed red pepper
   flakes
½ kosher dill pickle, cut into
   julienne strips

The dark meat of chicken and turkeys work best for barbecuing in the slow cooker. The white meat is too lean and dries out. Here I've used meaty turkey thighs, which are frequently on sale at my market. Another time, substitute the leg-thigh chicken quarters.

Pour ½ cup of the barbecue sauce into the bottom of a 5-quart or larger crockery slow cooker. Rinse the turkey; remove any fat. Pat dry with paper towels. Place the turkey in the cooker. Top with the onion and red pepper flakes. Pour the remaining barbecue sauce over all.

Cover and cook on LOW for 10 to 12 hours or on HIGH for 5 to 6 hours, until the turkey is tender. Transfer the turkey to a large, heated serving platter. Cut into portions. Keep warm. Pour the cooking juices into a large glass measuring cup. Skim off any fat that rises to the surface. Spoon the cooking juices over the turkey and sprinkle with the pickle. Serve immediately.

○ PER SERVING: 10 g carbohydrate (includes 1 g dietary fiber), 26 g protein, 13 g fat, 263 calories
○ DIABETIC EXCHANGES: 1 vegetable, 3½ lean meat, ½ fat

Duckling with Orange-Almond Sauce

I think duck is easier to cook in a slow cooker than in the oven, where it has a tendency to splatter grease. In a slow cooker, you have control of the fat that comes with this marvelous fowl. During the holiday season, I can buy fresh duck at my local supermarket. Other times of the year, I can either buy frozen or order a duck shipped by overnight air freight from the East Coast. This recipe is similar to the duck I was served off the coast from Seville, Spain, where many dishes come with the flavors of orange, sherry, and almonds.

MAKES 4 SERVINGS

1 (4-pound) ready-to-cook duck
2 oranges
1 small onion, peeled and
　　studded with 4 whole cloves
2 cloves garlic, peeled
Sweet paprika
1/8 teaspoon ground nutmeg
2 cups water
1/3 cup sugar-free orange
　　marmalade
2 tablespoons dry sherry or
　　fresh orange juice
1/2 cup sliced almonds

Rinse the duck and pat dry with paper towels. Using the tines of a fork, prick the skin all over the duck at 2-inch intervals. Slice one of the oranges (unpeeled) and place in the duck cavity, along with the onion and garlic cloves. Sprinkle the duck lightly with paprika and the nutmeg. Rub lightly into the skin. Place a wire rack or metal trivet in the bottom of a 5-quart or larger crockery slow cooker. Set the duck on the rack and pour the water into the cooker.

Cover and cook on LOW for 7 to 9 hours or on HIGH for 3½ to 4½ hours, until the meat near the thighbone is very tender when pierced. If possible, remove and discard the excess fat once or twice during the cooking time.

Before serving, transfer the duck to a shallow roasting pan and preheat the oven to 325°F. Roast the duck in the oven 15 to 20 minutes, until the skin is nicely browned and crisp. Transfer the duck to a heated carving platter. Let stand for 15 minutes before carving into pieces, discarding the skin. Discard the orange slices, onion, and garlic cloves from the cavity.

Meanwhile, working over a bowl to catch any juice, peel the remaining orange, removing and discarding all white pith. Release the orange segments, discarding the center membrane. In a small saucepan, combine any orange juice and the orange marmalade. Place over low heat and stir in the sherry. Heat until the marmalade is melted. Add the orange segments to the pan and cook, stirring occasionally, until the oranges are heated through, about 3 minutes. Stir in the almonds and transfer the sauce to a gravy boat to spoon over the duck. Carve the duck into 4 quarters and serve.

○ PER SERVING: 11 g carbohydrate (includes 1 g dietary fiber, 29 g protein, 11 g fat, 250 calories

○ DIABETIC EXCHANGES: ½ fruit, 4 lean meat, 1½ fat

Slow-Cooked Beef Roasts and Other Savory Meats

LARGE CUTS OF beef, pork, or lamb braised with fresh vegetables in a succulent sauce are easy to fix in a crockery slow cooker. Here you'll need to pay attention to the recipe and cut the vegetables as directed, for it takes a longer time to cook a whole carrot in a slow cooker than it does a big chunk of meat.

Many cooks, myself included, think pot roast is one of the best dishes produced in a slow cooker. I have offered ten recipes with tastes from all over the world, including the United States, France, Italy, Germany, and Mexico. There are also plenty of recipes for other cuts of beef, pork, and lamb. No matter which recipe you make, be sure the meat is very well trimmed so that the excess fat doesn't raise the temperature of the liquid as the meat cooks.

Beef Roast Slow-Cooked in Barola Wine

MAKES 6 SERVINGS

1 (2½-pound) boneless beef chuck roast, trimmed of fat

Salt and freshly ground pepper, to taste

1 tablespoon extra-virgin olive oil

2 medium carrots, peeled and finely chopped

1 medium onion, finely chopped

1 clove garlic, minced

1 medium rib celery, finely chopped

1 bottle Barola or other full-bodied tannic red wine

2 tablespoons tomato paste

1 sprig fresh rosemary

1 sprig fresh thyme

½ cinnamon stick

⅛ teaspoon ground cloves

½ cup brandy (optional)

The first time I tasted this classic of the Piedmont region, my husband and I were eating a late-night supper in a trattoria on the Italian side of Lake Maggiore. At the advice of our hotel concierge, we'd put ourselves in the hands of the chef/owner as to what we'd be eating. After delighting me with a plate of thin shavings of white truffle that he'd gathered that morning, with the simple embellishment of a drizzle of extra-virgin olive oil and a grinding of pepper, the chef introduced me to this perfect roast beef. The thin slices of tender beef were smothered in a rich wine sauce, with complex flavors including rosemary, wild mushrooms, and hints of cinnamon and clove. Served with grilled slices of polenta, it was one of the most memorable dishes ever.

Season the roast with salt and pepper. Heat the olive oil in a large nonstick skillet over medium-high heat. When the oil is hot but not smoking, add the roast and brown evenly on all

POT ROAST—AROUND THE WORLD IN FLAVOR

To my thinking, one of the foods that work best in a slow cooker is pot roast. With the slow, moist cooking, the toughest cuts of meat turn into a fork-tender delicacy. Watch your supermarket ads and when they offer a "lost leader" such as "buy one, get one free"—a sure enticement to get you into the market to buy more expensive items—stock up your freezer so that you always have the makings of a super main dish at hand. Although these recipes all begin with a pot roast, the flavors of the finished dishes are as varied as the world itself.

sides, 3 to 4 minutes per side.

Place the carrots, onion, garlic, and celery in the bottom of a 4-quart or larger crockery slow cooker. Add the beef. Combine the wine, tomato paste, rosemary, and thyme; pour over the beef. Add the cinnamon stick and cloves.

Cover and cook on LOW for 7 to 8 hours or on HIGH for 3½ to 4 hours, until the beef is tender. Transfer the beef to a carving board and let stand for 10 minutes before cutting against the grain into thin slices.

Meanwhile, transfer the pan juices to a saucepan and place over medium-high heat on top of the stove. Boil until reduced to about 2 cups, stirring frequently, and then add the brandy, if using. Continue to cook, stirring, for another 5 minutes.

Arrange the beef slices on a heated serving platter. Spoon the sauce over the beef and serve immediately.

○ PER SERVING: 6 g carbohydrate (includes 2 g dietary fiber), 36 g protein, 28 g fat, 454 calories
○ DIABETIC EXCHANGES: 1 vegetable, 5 lean meat, 2½ fat

SUBSTITUTES FOR ALCOHOL IN COOKING

Although some of the alcohol is eliminated in cooking, researchers have found that contrary to what was once thought, some of the alcohol remains even after prolonged cooking (see page 88). If you want to avoid using alcohol, here are some substitutions to consider:

For 1 cup (8 fluid ounces) of wine or spirits, use:

- an equal amount of nonalcoholic wine;

- ⅞ cup (7 fluid ounces) canned low-sodium chicken broth, beef broth, or vegetable broth and ⅛ cup (1 fluid ounce) fresh lemon juice;

- ⅞ cup (7 fluid ounces) water and ⅛ cup (1 fluid ounce) white or red wine vinegar, raspberry vinegar, or tarragon vinegar; or

- 1 cup water plus similarly flavored extract (such as rum extract or brandy extract).

Tuscan Pot Roast

As a rule, Tuscans don't eat a lot of beef, but when they do, it's won-derfully cooked with herbs and red wine. I've eaten their superb rendi-tion of pot roast prepared two ways and could only discern one difference in the recipes—the last time I had it, the cook had thrown a handful of golden raisins into the pot and garnished the finished dish with toasted pine nuts, which you can add or leave out.

Season the roast with salt and pepper. Heat the olive oil in a large nonstick skillet over medium-high heat. When hot but not smoking, add the roast and brown on all sides, about 5 min-utes per side.

Meanwhile, place the onions, garlic, carrot, and celery in the bottom of a 3½-quart or larger crockery slow cooker. Place the roast on top of the onions and add the tomatoes with juice, the rosemary, broth, and wine.

Cover and cook on LOW for 8 to 10 hours or on HIGH for 4 to 5 hours, until the roast is very tender when pierced with a fork. Transfer the roast to a carving board and keep warm. If necessary, skim and discard any fat from the cooking liquid. If cooking on LOW, increase the temperature setting to HIGH. Whisk in the dissolved cornstarch and, if using, the raisins and their soaking liquid. Cover and cook, stirring occasionally, until the sauce is thickened, 10 to 15 minutes.

To serve, slice the beef across the grain and arrange on a heated serving platter. Nap with the sauce and sprinkle with the pine nuts, if using, and the parsley.

○ PER SERVING: 15 g carbohydrate (includes 2 g dietary fiber), 34 g pro-tein, 25 g fat, 427 calories
○ DIABETIC EXCHANGES: 2 vegetable, 4½ lean meat, 2½ fat

MAKES 8 SERVINGS

1 (3-pound) boneless beef pot roast, such as chuck, rump, or round tip, trimmed of fat
Salt and freshly ground pepper, to taste
1 tablespoon extra-virgin olive oil
2 medium onions, chopped
3 cloves garlic, minced
1 medium carrot, peeled and finely minced
1 medium rib celery, finely minced
1 (28-ounce) can whole plum tomatoes, including juice
1 tablespoon minced fresh rosemary or 1 teaspoon crushed dried rosemary
3/4 cup canned low-sodium beef broth
3/4 cup dry red wine, preferably Chianti
2 tablespoons cornstarch, blended with 1/4 cup water
1/4 cup golden raisins, soaked in 1/4 cup brandy for 10 minutes (optional)
1/4 cup pine nuts, toasted (optional)
2 tablespoons chopped fresh flat-leaf parsley

Mediterranean Pot Roast

MAKES 8 SERVINGS

1 (3-pound) beef rump roast,
  trimmed of fat

Salt and freshly ground pepper,
  to taste

1 tablespoon extra-virgin olive
  oil

2 large onions, thinly sliced and
  separated into rings

2 cloves garlic, thinly sliced

1 (14½-ounce) can diced
  tomatoes, including juice

½ tablespoon grated orange
  zest

½ teaspoon crushed red pepper
  flakes

1 teaspoon ground cinnamon

¼ teaspoon ground ginger

1 cup canned low-sodium beef
  broth

1 cup pomegranate seeds

⅓ cup chopped walnuts

I love the flavor of this pot roast redolent with the flavors of the Mediterranean—sweet spices, garlic, citrus, and pomegranate. Since pomegranates are in season only for a few short months, I keep a bag of the sweet seeds in my freezer to use in cooking or as a garnish for salads and desserts. The seeds will separate easily when frozen.

Season the roast with salt and pepper. Heat the oil in a large nonstick skillet over medium-high heat. When the oil is hot but not smoking, add the roast and brown evenly on all sides, 3 to 4 minutes per side.

Place the onions and garlic in the bottom of a 4-quart or larger crockery slow cooker. Place the roast on top. Combine the tomatoes with juice, zest, red pepper flakes, cinnamon, ginger, and broth. Pour over the roast.

Cover and cook on LOW for 8 to 9 hours or on HIGH for 4 to 4½ hours, until the roast is fork-tender. Transfer the roast to a carving board and skim any fat from the pan juices.

Transfer the pan juices to a saucepot and boil on top of the stove over medium-high heat until the pan juices are reduced by half, about 5 minutes. Pour the mixture through a sieve, pressing the solids to extract their flavor and thicken the sauce. Return the strained sauce to the pan; discard the solids. Add the pomegranate seeds to the pan and simmer for 5 minutes.

Meanwhile, carve the roast against the grain into thin slices. Arrange the slices on a heated serving platter. Nap with the sauce and sprinkle with the walnuts.

○ PER SERVING: 10 g carbohydrate (includes 1 g dietary fiber), 33 g protein, 20 g fat, 335 calories

○ DIABETIC EXCHANGES: 1 vegetable, 4½ lean meat, 1½ fat

Sauerbraten

To properly develop its flavor, this German pot roast needs to marinate in the refrigerator for a day or two before cooking. Although it could do so in the crockery insert in the slow cooker, it will save refrigerator space to marinate the roast in a large self-sealing plastic bag.

Place the roast in a 1-gallon self-sealing heavy-duty plastic bag. In a large glass measuring cup, mix the vinegar, wine, brown sugar, dry mustard, allspice, cloves, and bay leaf. Pour over the roast in the bag. Add the onions, garlic, carrot, and celery. Seal the bag and refrigerate for 24 to 48 hours, turning the bag occasionally.

Remove the meat from the marinade and place in a 3½-quart or larger crockery slow cooker. If necessary, cut the roast into 2 pieces to fit. Place the marinade in a saucepan and bring to a full boil on top of the stove. Boil for 2 minutes. Pour the marinade into the slow cooker.

Cover and cook on LOW for 10 to 12 hours or on HIGH for 5 to 6 hours. Transfer the roast to a carving board. Strain the pan juices in a coarse sieve, pressing the solids with the back of a spoon to extract their liquid. Discard the solids and return 1 cup of the liquid to the slow cooker.

If cooking on LOW, increase the temperature setting to HIGH. Stir in the sour cream and gingersnaps. Cook, uncovered, for 10 minutes, until heated through and thickened. Do not boil.

To serve, carve the roast across the grain, spooning some of the gingersnap gravy over each serving.

○ PER SERVING: 16 g carbohydrate (includes 1 g dietary fiber), 34 g protein, 31 g fat, 482 calories
○ DIABETIC EXCHANGES: ½ bread/starch, ½ vegetable, 4½ lean meat, 3½ fat

MAKES 8 SERVINGS

1 (3-pound) boneless beef rump or chuck pot roast, trimmed of fat
½ cup cider vinegar
½ cup dry red wine
2 tablespoons light brown sugar
1 teaspoon dry mustard
¼ teaspoon ground allspice
⅛ teaspoon ground cloves
1 bay leaf
2 medium onions, thinly sliced
3 cloves garlic, thinly sliced
1 medium carrot, peeled and thinly sliced
1 medium rib celery with some leaves, chopped
Salt and freshly ground pepper, to taste
1 cup sour cream
½ cup crushed gingersnaps (about 12 cookies)

Yankee Pot Roast

MAKES 8 SERVINGS

2 teaspoons olive oil

1 (3-pound) tied boneless beef
chuck roast, trimmed of fat

Salt and freshly ground pepper,
to taste

1 large onion, coarsely chopped

1 small rutabaga, cut into 1-inch
pieces

2 medium ribs celery, thinly
sliced

3 medium carrots, peeled and
cut into 2-inch matchstick
lengths

4 medium plum tomatoes,
cored and sliced crosswise

1 cup low-sodium canned beef
broth

2 tablespoons tomato paste

1 tablespoon Worcestershire
sauce

Dash Tabasco sauce

1/2 teaspoon crushed dried
thyme

1 1/2 tablespoons cornstarch,
dissolved in 1/2 cup water

No one really knows the origin of this dish, and most every diner and homestyle restaurant in New England has its own version. This rendition is my particular favorite, similar to the pot roast that Orem's Diner, the gathering spot in my former Connecticut hometown, serves for Sunday dinner. The addition of Worcestershire sauce corrects the sweetness imparted by the vegetables.

Heat the oil in a large nonstick skillet over medium heat. Add the roast and cook on one side for 5 minutes. Sprinkle the roast with salt and pepper. Flip the roast and cook on the other side for an additional 5 minutes.

Meanwhile, place the onion, rutabaga, and celery in the bottom of a 4½-quart or larger crockery slow cooker. Place the roast on top of the vegetables and arrange the carrots and tomatoes around the roast. In a large glass measuring cup, whisk together the broth, tomato paste, Worcestershire sauce, Tabasco sauce, and thyme. Pour over the meat and vegetables.

Cover and cook on LOW for 8 to 10 hours or on HIGH for 4 to 5 hours, until the roast is very tender when pierced with a fork. Transfer the beef to a carving board and let stand for 15 minutes. If cooking on LOW, increase the cooking temperature to HIGH. Stir the dissolved cornstarch into the slow cooker and cook, uncovered, for 10 to 15 minutes, until the mixture thickens.

Carve the roast across the grain and arrange on a heated serving platter. Remove the vegetables with a slotted spoon and place on the platter. Nap with the pan sauce and serve.

○ PER SERVING: 9 g carbohydrate (includes 2 g dietary fiber), 33 g protein, 25 g fat, 398 calories

○ DIABETIC EXCHANGES: 1½ vegetable, 4½ lean meat, 2 fat

Wine Country Pot Roast with Root Vegetables

This dinner is a snap—fork-tender roast with a slew of vegetables that you put together in the morning to simmer all day while you're busy at work or just away from the kitchen. One of the main cook-friendly features of a slow cooker is the lack of precision necessary for this relaxed cooking method. If you're late arriving home, 30 minutes to an hour additional cooking won't matter. If you're cooking on HIGH and the dish is ready before you want to serve, just turn the setting to LOW to hold the food.

MAKES 8 SERVINGS

1 (3-pound) boneless beef chuck roast, trimmed of fat and tied

Salt and freshly ground pepper, to taste

1 tablespoon olive oil

1 large onion, chopped

3 cloves garlic, thinly sliced

3 medium carrots, peeled, cut lengthwise, and then cut into 2-inch pieces

3 medium white turnips, peeled and each cut into eighths

3 medium parsnips, peeled, cut lengthwise, and then into 2-inch pieces

1/2 teaspoon crushed dried thyme

1 bay leaf

1 cup Merlot or other dry red wine or canned low-sodium beef broth

2 tablespoons tomato paste

1 1/2 tablespoons cornstarch, dissolved in 2 tablespoons water

Season the roast with salt and pepper. Heat the oil in a large nonstick skillet over medium-high heat. When the oil is hot but not smoking, add the roast and brown on one side, about 5 minutes. Flip the roast over and brown on the other side for an additional 5 minutes.

Meanwhile, place the onion, garlic, carrots, turnips, and parsnips in the bottom of a 4½-quart or larger slow cooker. Transfer the roast to the cooker and place on top of the vegetables. Sprinkle with the thyme and add the bay leaf. Pour the wine into the skillet used to brown the beef and stir with a wooden spoon to loosen any browned bits from the bottom of the skillet. Whisk in the tomato paste and pour the mixture over the roast.

Cover and cook on LOW 8 to 9 hours or on HIGH for 4 to 5½ hours, until the roast is tender when pierced with a fork. Transfer the roast to a carving board and let stand for 15 minutes. Remove the vegetables with a slotted spoon and arrange on a heated serving platter.

Meanwhile, if cooking on LOW, increase the temperature setting to HIGH. Skim off and discard any fat on the cooking surface in the cooker. Whisk the dissolved cornstarch into the slow cooker and cook on HIGH for another 10 to 15 minutes, until the pan sauce is bubbling. Pour the sauce into a gravy boat to spoon over the meat and vegetables.

Slice the meat across the grain and arrange the slices on the serving platter. Serve immediately.

○ PER SERVING: 18 g carbohydrate (includes 4 g dietary fiber), 34 g protein, 21 g fat, 410 calories
○ DIABETIC EXCHANGES: 3 vegetable, 4$\frac{1}{2}$ lean meat, 1$\frac{1}{2}$ fat

Sunday Pot Roast Dinner

This kind of pot roast was frequent Sunday dinner fare in my mother's kitchen. Cooked slowly on top of the stove, the roast needed frequent checking to make sure that it didn't cook dry. A slow cooker eliminates that possibility, and peeking at the cooking roast is even discouraged. This is a "cook it and forget it" kind of recipe.

If necessary, cut the roast into 2 pieces to fit into a 3½-quart or larger crockery slow cooker. Season the roast with salt and pepper; sprinkle with the flour. Heat the oil in a large skillet over medium-high heat. Add the roast and brown on all sides, about 10 minutes total.

Meanwhile, place the onions, carrots, celery, and garlic in the slow cooker. Place the roast on top. Lay the bay leaves and parsley bundle on top of the roast. In a large measuring cup, combine the tomato sauce, wine, and thyme. Pour over the roast and vegetables.

Cover and cook on LOW for 10 to 12 hours or on HIGH for 5 to 6 hours, until the roast is tender when pierced with a fork. During the last 30 minutes of cooking time on LOW (15 minutes on HIGH), stir the cabbage into the pan liquids. Continue to cook, covered, until the cabbage is tender.

Transfer the roast to a carving board. Let rest for 10 minutes, then slice across the grain. Arrange the sliced roast on a large heated serving platter. Spoon the vegetables and pan juices around the meat, discarding the bay leaves and parsley bundle. Serve immediately.

○ **PER SERVING:** 21 g carbohydrate (includes 3 g dietary fiber), 39 g protein, 28 g fat, 498 calories

○ **DIABETIC EXCHANGES:** 3½ vegetable, 5 lean meat, 3 fat

MAKES 6 SERVINGS

1 (2½-pound) boneless beef chuck pot roast, trimmed of fat

Salt and freshly ground pepper, to taste

2 tablespoons unbleached all-purpose flour

1 tablespoon canola oil

2 medium onions, thinly sliced

4 medium carrots, peeled and thinly sliced

4 medium ribs celery, thinly sliced

2 cloves garlic, thinly sliced

2 bay leaves

½ bunch parsley, stems tied together with kitchen string

1 (15-ounce) can tomato sauce

¼ cup robust red wine or water

¼ teaspoon crushed dried thyme

1 small head cabbage, cored and coarsely chopped

Dry-Rubbed Beef Brisket

Dry Rub

1 teaspoon chili powder

1 teaspoon light brown sugar

$^1/_2$ teaspoon garlic powder

$^1/_2$ teaspoon sweet Hungarian
    paprika

$^1/_4$ teaspoon lemon pepper
    seasoning

$^1/_4$ teaspoon dry mustard

$^1/_4$ teaspoon onion powder

$^1/_4$ teaspoon crushed dried
    thyme

$^1/_8$ teaspoon ground ginger

1 (3-pound) beef brisket, well
    trimmed of fat

$^1/_2$ cup water

$^1/_2$ teaspoon liquid smoke

Whenever I ask someone what their favorite slow cooker recipe, more than half mention a brisket—a cut of beef that requires slow cooking to tenderize it and bring out its flavor. Ask your butcher for the flat-cut, often referred to as "first cut" brisket.

To make the rub: Combine all the ingredients in a small bowl.

Rub the dry rub into both sides of the brisket. Place a wire rack or metal trivet in a 3½-quart or larger crockery slow cooker. Combine the water and liquid smoke. Pour into the slow cooker. Place the brisket on the rack. If necessary, cut the brisket into 2 pieces to fit.

Cover and cook on LOW for 7½ to 9½ hours or on HIGH for 4 to 5 hours, until the brisket is fork-tender.

Lift the brisket from the cooker and let stand for 20 minutes. Slice the brisket very thinly or shred.

○ PER SERVING: 1 g carbohydrate (includes trace dietary fiber), 7 g fat, 221 calories
○ DIABETIC EXCHANGES: 5 lean meat

VARIATION

Barbecued Brisket

To make barbecued brisket, follow the recipe above. Pour off any pan juices in the slow cooker. Return the sliced or shredded beef to the cooker. Add 2½ cups Aunt Miriam's Barbecue Sauce (see page 129) to the cooker and stir to combine. Cover and continue to cook on HIGH for 12 to 20 minutes, until heated through.

○ PER SERVING (5 OUNCES BRISKET PLUS $^1/_4$ CUP SAUCE): 7 g carbohydrate (includes 1 g dietary fiber), 36 g protein, 8 g fat, 252 calories
○ DIABETIC EXCHANGES: $^1/_2$ vegetable, 5 lean meat

Aunt Miriam's Barbecue Sauce

Growing up, I loved to fly to my Aunt Miriam's home in Oklahoma for a summer visit. She doted on me and introduced me to lots of exotic food flavors. Knowing I loved her barbecue sauce on most everything, she'd always make it on my first day there, simmering it on the stove for hours and frequently stirring and checking on its progress. I recently found her hand-written recipe in her kitchen notebook, which I inherited. Here it's adapted for a crockery slow cooker. It requires no attention during the 4 to 5 hours that it's cooking. Since orange marmalade is now available sugar-free, it cuts down on the carbs.

MAKES ABOUT 5 CUPS

1 tablespoon canola oil
1 medium onion, chopped
2 cloves garlic, minced
1 (8-ounce) can tomato sauce
1 cup ketchup
1 cup canned low-sodium beef broth
1/4 cup cider vinegar
1/4 cup fresh lemon juice
1/4 cup sugar-free orange marmalade
2 tablespoons frozen orange juice concentrate
2 tablespoons Worcestershire sauce
1/2 tablespoon sweet Hungarian paprika
1/2 tablespoon chili powder
1 teaspoon salt
1/4 teaspoon crushed dried oregano

Heat the oil in a large nonstick skillet over medium heat. Add the onion and garlic and sauté until limp, about 5 minutes. Transfer to a 3-quart slow cooker and combine with the remaining ingredients. Cover and cook on LOW for 4 to 5 hours.

Cool and transfer to sterilized glass jars. Cover and refrigerate for up to 3 to 4 weeks. Use to spoon over any cuts of beef, lamb, pork, or poultry as they cook in a slow cooker or on a grill.

○ PER 1/4-CUP SERVING (SAUCE ONLY): 7 g carbohydrate (includes 1 g dietary fiber), 1 g protein, 1 g fat, 31 calories
○ DIABETIC EXCHANGES: 1 vegetable

Santa Fe Roast

MAKES 10 SERVINGS

1 (3-pound) boneless beef eye of
round, trimmed of fat

Salt and freshly ground pepper,
to taste

1 tablespoon extra-virgin olive
oil

2 large onions, thinly sliced and
separated into rings

2 large red bell peppers, cut
into julienne strips

1 (28-ounce) can plum tomatoes
with juice, coarsely chopped

½ cup canned low-sodium beef
broth

2 serrano chiles, seeded and
minced

1 teaspoon ground cumin

1 teaspoon crushed dried
oregano

½ teaspoon crushed dried
thyme

½ teaspoon sweet paprika

2 tablespoons chopped fresh
cilantro

*While not technically a pot roast, the beef eye of round is very tender
and succulent when cooked by moist heat like a pot roast. I would
spend a few more carbs and serve this richly flavored roast with
warmed black beans to complete the meal.*

Season the roast with salt and pepper. In a large nonstick skillet,
heat the oil over medium-high heat. Add the roast and brown
on all sides, about 5 minutes total.

Meanwhile, place the onions and bell peppers in the bottom of a 4-quart or larger crockery slow cooker. Place the roast
on top. In a large bowl, combine the tomatoes with juice, broth,
chiles, cumin, oregano, thyme, and paprika. Pour over the roast.

Cover and cook on LOW for 8 to 9 hours or on HIGH for
4 to 4½ hours. Transfer the roast to a carving board and keep
warm. If cooking on LOW, increase the cooking temperature to
HIGH. Cook the vegetables and pan juices, uncovered, for 10
minutes to reduce slightly.

Cut the roast on the diagonal into thin slices. Arrange on a
heated serving platter and spoon the vegetables and some of the
pan juices over the roast. Sprinkle with the cilantro and serve
immediately.

○ PER SERVING: 11 g carbohydrate (includes 2 g dietary fiber), 38 g protein, 13 g fat, 316 calories

○ DIABETIC EXCHANGES: 2 vegetable, 5 lean meat

Mexican Pot Roast with Mexican Vegetables

Nothing depicts a celebration of life better than sharing a meal with family or friends. Such has been the case every time we dine with our friends from south of the border—delicious food, whether hot with chiles or not, that delights our taste buds and seduces us to linger at the table late into the night. Such is the case of this pot roast that is slow cooked Mexican style.

Every year when the Hatch chiles arrive in my local market from New Mexico, I order a year's supply to be roasted and freeze them in small batches in self-sealing plastic freezer bags to use in dishes such as this. You could also roast some fresh poblano chiles or use canned green chiles.

MAKES 8 SERVINGS

1 tablespoon canola oil

1 (3-pound) boneless beef chuck roast, trimmed of fat

1 cup water

1 large onion, cut in half and thinly sliced

3 cloves garlic, cut into thin slivers

5 roasted mild green chiles, seeded and cut into lengthwise strips (see recipe headnote)

3 large plum tomatoes, cored and coarsely chopped

2 medium chayotes, peeled, pitted, and coarsely chopped

1 teaspoon crushed dried oregano, preferably Mexican

1/2 teaspoon crushed dried thyme

1 cup frozen corn kernels

Heat the oil in a heavy nonstick skillet over medium–high heat. Add the roast and brown all sides, about 10 minutes. Add the water to the skillet and scrape the bottom of the pan with a wooden spoon to loosen any browned bits.

Meanwhile, place the onion, garlic, and chiles in the bottom of a 4½-quart or larger crockery slow cooker. Transfer the roast and the pan juices to the cooker. Distribute the tomatoes and chayotes around the roast and sprinkle with the oregano and thyme.

Cover and cook on LOW for 7 to 8 hours or on HIGH for 3½ to 4 hours, until the roast is very tender when pierced with a fork. If cooking on LOW, increase the temperature setting to HIGH. Transfer the roast to a carving board and let stand for 15 minutes.

Add the corn to the cooker, cover, and cook for another 10 to 15 minutes, until the corn is just tender. To serve, slice the beef across the grain and arrange on a heated serving platter. Using a slotted spoon, transfer the vegetables to the serving platter and arrange around the roast. Pour any pan juices into a gravy boat to spoon over each serving. Serve immediately.

○ PER SERVING: 12 g carbohydrate (includes 3 g dietary fiber), 34 g protein, 25 g fat, 412 calories
○ DIABETIC EXCHANGES: 1$\frac{1}{2}$ vegetable, 4$\frac{1}{2}$ lean meat, 2 fat

Braciola with Tomato Sauce

Braciola (stuffed beef bundles) is one of my favorite Italian beef dishes—a dish that adapts well to the slow cooker. The dish is made even easier by using a jar of spaghetti sauce. Of course, if you happen to have a container of your own homemade meatless sauce in the freezer, by all means use that.

MAKES 4 SERVINGS

1¼ pounds boneless beef top round steak

Salt and freshly ground pepper, to taste

4 (1-ounce) slices mozzarella cheese

½ cup freshly grated Parmesan cheese

2 cloves garlic, minced

2 tablespoons dried currants

2 cups tomato-basil meatless spaghetti sauce (see headnote)

1 tablespoon balsamic vinegar

½ teaspoon crushed red pepper flakes, or to taste

1 tablespoon capers, rinsed and drained

2 tablespoons pine nuts, toasted

Place the steak on a work surface and cut into 4 equal pieces. Lightly season with salt and pepper. Lay a slice of mozzarella cheese on top of each piece of steak. Sprinkle with the Parmesan cheese, garlic, and currants. Roll up, jelly-roll style, and tie each bundle 2 or 3 times with kitchen string. Place the bundles, seam-side down, in a 3½-quart or larger crockery slow cooker. Cover with the spaghetti sauce.

Cover and cook on LOW for 6 to 7 hours or on HIGH for 3 to 3½ hours. Transfer the beef bundles to a heated serving platter. If cooking on LOW, increase the temperature setting to HIGH. Stir in the vinegar, red pepper flakes, and capers. Cook, uncovered, for 5 minutes and spoon over the beef bundles. Sprinkle with the pine nuts and serve.

○ **PER SERVING:** 18 g carbohydrate (includes 3 g dietary fiber), 46 g protein, 19 g fat, 433 calories

○ **DIABETIC EXCHANGES:** 1 bread/starch, 6½ lean meat

Mandarin Broccoli Beef

MAKES 6 SERVINGS

2 pounds lean boneless beef top
round steak, cut into thin
strips

1 large red bell pepper, cut into
julienne strips

3 inner ribs celery, thinly sliced
on the diagonal

6 scallions, white part and 1
inch green, thinly sliced

2 tablespoons minced fresh
ginger

3 tablespoons reduced-sodium
soy sauce

1 tablespoon oyster sauce

⅓ cup dry red wine or rice
vinegar

½ teaspoon crushed red pepper
flakes

3 cups broccoli florets

1 tablespoon cornstarch, mixed
with 2 tablespoons water
(optional)

1 (6-ounce) can mandarin
oranges, drained

Fresh ginger and soy sauce permeate the beef steak, while canned mandarin oranges offer a delightful color contract to the mahogany sauce. If you can spare the carbs, serve this with steamed brown rice. Otherwise, serve it on a bed of shredded lettuce.

In a 3½-quart or larger crockery slow cooker, combine all of the ingredients through the broccoli.

Cover and cook on LOW for 8 to 10 hours or on HIGH for 4 to 5 hours. During the last 30 minutes of cooking time, add the broccoli and stir in to combine.

If a thicker sauce is desired, remove the steak and broccoli and whisk in the dissolved cornstarch. Cook, stirring, uncovered, until the mixture has thickened. Return the steak and broccoli to the cooker and stir in the mandarin oranges. Serve hot.

○ PER SERVING: 11 g carbohydrate (includes 2 g dietary fiber), 37 g protein, 6 g fat, 252 calories

○ DIABETIC EXCHANGES: 1½ vegetable, 5 very lean meat

Mongolian Beef

This recipe is inspired by the fare offered at a new Mongolian Grill near my home, where they garnish your dish with stir-fried cilantro and scallions for a spike of flavor.

In a 3½-quart or larger crockery slow cooker, combine the tomatoes with their juice, red onion, garlic, ginger, red pepper flakes, and turmeric. Add the beef and toss to combine. Pour the broth and soy sauce into the cooker.

Cover and cook on LOW for 7 to 9 hours or on HIGH for 3½ to 4½ hours. If cooking on LOW, increase the cooking temperature to HIGH. Stir in the baby corn and continue to cook until corn is heated through, about 5 minutes.

Heat the oil in a large nonstick skillet. Add the cilantro and scallions. Stir-fry for 1 to 2 minutes, until lightly browned and fragrant. Watch carefully and do not burn. Transfer the beef and vegetables with sauce to a serving dish. Sprinkle with the cilantro and scallions. Serve immediately.

○ PER SERVING: 12 g carbohydrate (includes 2 g dietary fiber), 31 g protein, 21 g fat, 357 calories
○ DIABETIC EXCHANGES: ½ bread/starch, 1 vegetable, 4 lean meat, 1½ fat

MAKES 6 SERVINGS

1 (14½-ounce) can plum tomatoes, including juice
½ cup finely chopped red onion
3 cloves garlic, minced
2 teaspoons grated fresh ginger
2 to 3 teaspoons crushed red pepper flakes, or to taste
¼ teaspoon turmeric
2 pounds lean boneless beef top sirloin, trimmed of fat and cut into 1-inch strips
1 cup canned low-sodium beef broth
2 tablespoons reduced-sodium soy sauce
1 (6-ounce) jar baby corn on the cob, drained
1 tablespoon canola oil
½ cup fresh cilantro leaves, coarsely chopped
½ cup chopped scallions

Slow-Cooker Steak with Portobello Mushrooms

MAKES 6 SERVINGS

2 pounds ¾-inch-thick lean top
   beef round steak

1 tablespoon Worcestershire
   sauce

Freshly ground pepper, to taste

¾ cup finely chopped shallots
   or red onion

1 tablespoon butter, melted

1 pound portobello mushrooms,
   cleaned

½ cup canned low-sodium beef
   broth

2 tablespoons fresh lemon juice

1 tablespoon Dijon mustard

2 teaspoons dry mustard

⅓ cup heavy cream

2 tablespoons brandy (optional)

2 tablespoons minced fresh
   parsley

Reminiscent in flavor to steak Diane, this slow-cooker steak also features meaty portobello mushrooms. Serve this luxurious main dish with sautéed fresh spinach and cauliflower mashed with butter and a dash of heavy cream.

Trim all fat from the steak and cut into 6 equal pieces. Brush the steak with the Worcestershire sauce and season with pepper. Toss the shallots with the butter and place in the bottom of a 4-quart or larger crockery slow cooker. Place the steak pieces on top of the shallots.

Remove the mushroom stems and reserve for another use. Slice the caps and place on top of the steak. In a glass measuring cup, whisk together the beef broth, lemon juice, Dijon mustard, and dry mustard. Pour over the steak and mushrooms.

Cover and cook on LOW for 8 to 10 hours or on HIGH for 4 to 5 hours. Transfer the steak to a warm serving platter. If cooking on LOW, increase the temperature setting to HIGH. Stir the cream and brandy (if using) into the slow cooker. Cook, stirring frequently, for 10 minutes. Spoon the mushrooms and sauce over the steak and sprinkle with the parsley. Serve immediately.

○ **PER SERVING:** 8 g carbohydrate (includes 1 g dietary fiber), 38 g protein, 13 g fat, 306 calories
○ **DIABETIC EXCHANGES:** 1 vegetable, 5 lean meat

Pepper Steak

You can buy frozen strips of peppers with onion to make this very easy dish. Boneless chuck steak is less expensive than top round or top sirloin and cooks to tender perfection in the slow cooker.

Trim the fat from the steak and cut into 8 serving portions. Season the steak with salt and pepper. Place the meat in a 3½-quart or larger crockery slow cooker. In a medium bowl, combine the tomatoes with juice, the tomato paste, onion soup mix, and Worcestershire sauce. Pour over the steak. Top with the vegetables.

Cover and cook on LOW for 10 to 12 hours or on HIGH for 5 to 6 hours. If using, serve with hot cooked pasta.

○ PER SERVING (STEAK AND VEGETABLES ONLY): 17 g carbohydrate (includes 3 g dietary fiber), 46 g protein, 17 g fat, 404 calories
○ DIABETIC EXCHANGES: 2½ vegetable, 6 lean meat

MAKES 6 SERVINGS

2 pounds ¾-inch-thick boneless beef chuck steak

Salt and freshly ground pepper, to taste

1 (14½-ounce) can stewed tomatoes, including juice

1 (6-ounce) can tomato paste

1 envelope (½ of a 2.2-ounce package) dry onion soup mix

2 tablespoons Worcestershire sauce

1 (16-ounce) package frozen pepper stir-fry vegetables (yellow, green, and red bell peppers with onion)

Hot cooked whole wheat pasta (optional)

Country Swiss Steak

MAKES 6 SERVINGS

2½ tablespoons all-purpose flour

1 teaspoon dry mustard

½ teaspoon crushed dried thyme

¼ teaspoon sweet paprika

2 pounds 1-inch-thick boneless beef top round steak

1½ tablespoons Worcestershire sauce

Salt and freshly ground pepper, to taste

1 tablespoon canola oil

1 clove garlic, minced

2 medium ribs celery, thinly sliced

2 medium onion, thinly sliced

6 large plum tomatoes, thinly sliced crosswise

½ cup canned low-sodium beef broth

This is the way my mother cooked Swiss steak. Made in a slow cooker, it's fork tender and exceptionally delicious.

In a small bowl, combine the flour, dry mustard, thyme, and paprika. Set aside. Cut the steak into 6 serving pieces. Brush the steak pieces with the Worcestershire sauce and season with salt and pepper. Sprinkle the flour-herb mixture over the steak and press the flour into the steak with your fingers.

Heat the oil in a large nonstick skillet over medium-high heat. Add the steak and brown for 5 minutes per side, turning once. Transfer the steak to a 3½-quart crockery slow cooker. Sprinkle with the garlic and top with the celery, onion, and tomatoes. Pour in the broth.

Cover and cook on LOW for 6 to 8 hours or on HIGH for 3 to 4 hours, until the steak is tender. If cooking on HIGH, stir once during the last hour of cooking.

To serve, transfer the steak and vegetables to a heated serving platter. Spoon on any pan juices and serve.

O PER SERVING: 11 g carbohydrate (includes 2 g dietary fiber), 36 g protein, 9 g fat, 273 calories

O DIABETIC EXCHANGES: 1½ vegetable, 5 lean meat

Curried Beef

Another superb recipe from my friend Pat Eby, one of Reno's best cooks. Because Pat's days are filled with community and charity work, she likes this kind of dish at the ready on nights that she's entertaining guests for dinner.

Place the onions, ginger, and garlic in a 4-quart or larger crockery slow cooker. Mix together the cumin, coriander, turmeric, paprika, cloves, cayenne, and nutmeg. Sprinkle over the onion mixture. Add the cinnamon stick to the cooker. Toss the beef with the flour and place in the cooker. Mix together the tomato paste and water. Pour over the beef.

Cover and cook on LOW for 8 to 9 hours or on HIGH for 4 to 4½ hours. Stir in the cilantro. Taste and add salt and pepper, if needed. Transfer the beef and sauce to a heated serving dish. Sprinkle with the peanuts and scallions. Serve at once.

○ PER SERVING: 11 g carbohydrate (includes 2 g dietary fiber), 43 g protein, 12 g fat, 321 calories
○ DIABETIC EXCHANGES: 1 vegetable, 6 lean meat

MAKES 8 SERVINGS

2 large onions, finely chopped
3 tablespoons grated fresh
   ginger
6 cloves garlic, minced
2 tablespoons ground cumin
1 tablespoon ground coriander
1 teaspoon turmeric
1 teaspoon sweet paprika
½ teaspoon ground cloves
½ teaspoon cayenne pepper
¼ teaspoon ground nutmeg
1 (4-inch) cinnamon stick
3 pounds boneless lean beef top
   round, cut into 1 × ½-inch
   strips
3 tablespoons all-purpose flour
⅓ cup tomato paste
⅔ cup water
⅓ cup chopped fresh cilantro
Salt and freshly ground pepper,
   to taste
½ cup roasted peanuts
½ cup thinly sliced scallions,
   including some green

Slow-Cooked Tamale Pie

MAKES 10 SERVINGS

2 (15-ounce) cans beef tamales

1 pound extra-lean ground beef sirloin

1 medium onion, chopped

1 large red bell pepper, chopped

½ cup mild or hot taco sauce

1 (15-ounce) can black beans, rinsed and drained

1 (14½-ounce) can plum tomatoes, coarsely chopped, including juice

1 (4-ounce) can diced green chiles, drained

1 (4-ounce) can sliced black olives, drained

½ cup grated cheddar cheese

½ cup grated Monterey Jack cheese

⅔ cup sour cream, for garnish (optional)

½ cup chopped scallions, for garnish (optional)

Although certainly inspired by Mexican tamales, tamale pie is a Western dish. I have an old community recipe book published by a Los Angeles church group in 1932 that has a recipe for tamale pie. This version comes from my sister-in-law Gloria Giedt, a marvelous and innovative cook. If your market features freshly made tamales, use 4 large beef tamales instead of the two cans.

Unwrap the tamales and cut into slices. Lay half of the tamale slices in the bottom of a 5-quart or larger crockery slow cooker.

In a large nonstick skillet, brown the beef over medium-high heat, stirring occasionally, about 5 minutes. Drain off any fat and stir in the onion and bell pepper. Remove from the heat and stir in the taco sauce, black beans, tomatoes with juice, the chiles, and olives. Spoon this mixture on top of the tamales. Place the remaining tamale slices on top.

Cover and cook on LOW for 6 to 7 hours. Sprinkle the cheeses on top and cook, covered, another 5 minutes, until the cheese melts. Scoop out servings with a large spoon. If using, garnish each serving with a dollop of sour cream and a sprinkling of the scallions.

○ PER SERVING: 23 g carbohydrate (includes 5 g dietary fiber), 17 g protein, 10 g fat, 242 calories

○ DIABETIC EXCHANGES: 1 carbohydrate (½ bread/starch, 1½ vegetable), 1 very lean protein, ½ lean protein, ½ fat

Asian-Style Beef Short Ribs

A slow-cooker renders these short ribs fork-tender. Try this recipe when you have a house full of guests. They'll wonder how such a great cooking aroma could be wafting from the kitchen when you're relaxing with them. Look for the five-spice powder in the spice aisle of your supermarket.

Preheat the broiler. Arrange the short ribs on the broiler pan and broil for 5 minutes per side, turning once, to lightly brown and remove any fat.

Place the leeks and garlic in the bottom of a 5-quart or larger crockery slow cooker. In a large glass measuring cup, whisk together the soy sauce, broth, sesame seeds, brown sugar, lemon zest, five-spice powder, and pepper. Pour over the short ribs.

Cover and cook on LOW for 7 to 8 hours or on HIGH for 3½ to 4 hours. Transfer the short ribs and the pan sauce to a heated serving platter. Sprinkle with the scallions and serve immediately.

○ PER SERVING: 10 g carbohydrate (includes 1 g dietary fiber), 33 g protein, 20 g fat, 354 calories
○ DIABETIC EXCHANGES: 1 vegetable, 4½ lean meat, 1 fat

MAKES 8 SERVINGS

3 pounds lean boneless beef short ribs, trimmed of fat
3 leeks, trimmed, white part and 1 inch green, well washed, and thinly sliced
4 cloves garlic, minced
¼ cup reduced-sodium soy sauce
½ cup canned low-sodium beef broth
2 tablespoons sesame seeds
1 tablespoon light brown sugar
2 teaspoons grated lemon zest
1 teaspoon Chinese five-spice powder
½ teaspoon freshly ground pepper
¼ cup chopped scallions, including some green tops

Yankee Short Ribs

MAKES 8 SERVINGS

4 pounds boneless beef short
    ribs, cut about 3 inches long
    and trimmed of fat

Salt and freshly ground pepper,
    to taste

1 large orange

1 large onion, finely chopped

4 cloves garlic, minced

12 dried apricots, cut into thin
    slices

1 cup canned low-sodium beef
    broth

½ cup dry red wine

2 tablespoons balsamic vinegar

2 tablespoons reduced-sodium
    soy sauce

1 teaspoon crushed dried thyme

¼ cup thinly sliced scallions,
    white part and 1 inch green

When we lived in Connecticut, I frequently took these meaty short ribs to potluck suppers. Drenched in a savory sauce, they never failed to make a hit. If your market sells Turkish dried apricots, by all means use them—they are far superior to domestic dried ones.

Season the short ribs with salt and pepper. Place in the bottom of a 5-quart or larger crockery slow cooker. Using a zester or vegetable peeler, remove the zest from the orange, leaving the white pith. Reserve the orange for another use. Cut the zest into thin slivers and combine with the rest of the ingredients *except* the scallions. Pour over the ribs.

Cover and cook on LOW for 10 to 12 hours or on HIGH for 5 to 6 hours, until the meat is very tender when pierced with a fork. Transfer the ribs to a heated serving platter and keep warm. If cooking on LOW, increase the temperature setting to HIGH. Cook, uncovered, until the sauce is reduced to about 1 cup, 10 to 15 minutes. Pour the pan sauce over the ribs and sprinkle with the scallions. Serve immediately.

○ **PER SERVING:** 11 g carbohydrate (includes 1 g dietary fiber), 32 g protein, 18 g fat, 342 calories

○ **DIABETIC EXCHANGES:** ½ fruit, 4½ lean meat, 1 fat

Short Ribs Jardinière

These delectable short ribs are easy to make. Serve them with mashed cauliflower or turnips and a tossed green salad.

In a large nonstick skillet, heat the oil over medium–high heat. Add the short ribs and brown on all sides, turning occasionally, for about 10 minutes. Transfer the ribs to the bottom of a 4-quart or larger crockery slow cooker. In the same skillet, sauté the onion, garlic, and celery until the vegetables are limp, about 4 minutes. Spoon the vegetables over the ribs. Add the tomatoes with juice, the broth, and Italian seasoning.

Cover and cook on LOW for 8 to 10 hours or on HIGH for 4 to 5 hours. Transfer the ribs to a heated serving platter. Spoon the pan sauce and vegetables over the ribs. Sprinkle with the parsley and serve immediately.

○ PER SERVING: 6 g carbohydrate (includes 1 g dietary fiber), 32 g protein, 20 g fat, 342 calories

○ DIABETIC EXCHANGES: 1 vegetable, 4½ lean meat, 1 fat

MAKES 6 SERVINGS

1 tablespoon extra-virgin olive oil

3 pounds lean boneless beef short ribs, trimmed of fat

1 cup chopped onion

1 clove garlic, minced

⅓ cup chopped celery

1 (14½-ounce) can plum tomatoes, coarsely chopped, including juice

½ cup canned low-sodium beef broth

1 teaspoon crushed dried Italian herb seasoning

2 tablespoons chopped parsley

Low-Carb Meat Loaf

MAKES 6 SERVINGS

1½ pounds lean ground beef
round

½ pound ground veal

1 medium green bell pepper,
finely diced

1 medium onion, finely diced

2 cloves garlic, minced

1 medium rib celery, finely
diced

⅓ cup freshly grated Parmesan
cheese

1 teaspoon crushed dried
Italian herb seasoning

1 large egg

2 tablespoons tomato-based
chili sauce

1 tablespoon Worcestershire
sauce

⅛ to ¼ teaspoon Tabasco sauce

3 slices lean bacon

For years, my California neighbor and I exchanged recipes over the backyard fence. When I was put on a low-carb diet back in the spring of 1970, I was particularly thrilled to get her mother-in-law's recipe for meat loaf. The recipe has changed considerably over the years, but it's still low in carbs.

In a large bowl, combine the beef, veal, bell pepper, onion, garlic, celery, Parmesan cheese, and Italian seasoning. In a measuring cup, beat together the egg, chili sauce, Worcestershire sauce, and Tabasco sauce. Add to the beef mixture and mix well. Form the mixture into an 8-inch round loaf. Place a wire rack or trivet in the bottom of a 5-quart or larger crockery slow cooker, and place the loaf on the rack.

Cover and cook on LOW for 7 to 9 hours or on HIGH for 3½ to 4½ hours, until an instant-read thermometer registers 170°F in the center of the loaf. Transfer the loaf to a heated serving platter and cut into 8 wedges to serve.

○ **PER SERVING:** 5 g carbohydrate (includes 1 g dietary fiber), 33 g protein, 21 g fat, 353 calories

○ **DIABETIC EXCHANGES:** ½ vegetable, 4½ lean meat, 2 fat

Mexican Meat Loaf

This makes a delicious, moist loaf. Serve the wedges on a bed of shredded lettuce as the focal point of a south-of-the-border meal. Pass salsa and sour cream to spoon on top.

In a large mixing bowl, combine the beef, eggs, milk, oats, olives, tomatoes with juice, celery, onion, garlic, chipotle chiles, cumin, and cheese. Add 1 cup of the salsa and mix well. Form into an 8-inch round loaf. Place a wire rack or trivet in the bottom of a 5-quart or larger crockery slow cooker, and place the meat loaf on the rack.

Cover and cook on LOW for 7 to 9 hours or on HIGH for 3½ to 4½ hours, until an instant-read thermometer registers 170°F in the center of the loaf. Transfer the loaf to a heated serving platter and let stand for 10 minutes. Cut the loaf into 8 wedges.

Place a pile of shredded lettuce on each of 8 dinner plates. Place a wedge of the meat loaf on top. Top each with a spoonful of the reserved salsa and a small spoonful of sour cream. Serve immediately.

O **PER SERVING:** 19 g carbohydrate (includes 3 g dietary fiber), 39 g protein, 19 g fat, 386 calories

O **DIABETIC EXCHANGES:** 2 vegetable, 4½ lean meat

MAKES 6 SERVINGS

2 pounds extra lean ground beef, preferably sirloin

2 large eggs

¾ cup 2% low-fat milk

½ cup quick-cooking rolled oats

16 large brine-cured black olives, pitted and thinly sliced

1 (10-ounce) can tomatoes with green chiles, including juice

½ cup finely diced celery

½ cup finely diced onion

1 clove garlic, minced

1 to 2 tablespoons chopped canned chipotle chiles in adobo sauce, or to taste

½ teaspoon ground cumin

½ cup shredded Monterey Jack cheese

2 cups mild or hot purchased fresh salsa, divided

4 cups shredded lettuce

½ cup sour cream

Veal Shanks with Lemon and Parsley

MAKES 4 SERVINGS

4 (3-inch) meaty veal shanks
(about 4 pounds)
Salt and freshly ground pepper,
to taste
1 tablespoon extra-virgin olive
oil
1 medium onion, minced
1 medium rib celery with some
leaves, minced
1 medium carrot, peeled and
minced
1 clove garlic, minced
4 large plum tomatoes, seeded
and minced
2 cups canned low-sodium
chicken broth
2 tablespoons tomato paste
½ teaspoon crushed dried basil
½ teaspoon crushed dried
oregano

Lemon and Parsley Garnish
⅓ cup minced parsley
Grated zest of 1 lemon
1 clove garlic, minced

Also known as osso buco, meaty, slow-cooked tender veal shanks are one of life's great dining pleasures. A crockery slow cooker does this dish to perfection, but don't try this recipe on a HIGH setting. The veal needs to simmer "low and slow" to completely develop its full flavor. The veal shanks are large, so you'll need a 5-quart or larger cooker; if you only have a 3½- or 4-quart cooker, halve the recipe.

Season the veal shanks with salt and pepper. Heat the oil in a large nonstick skillet over medium-high heat. Add the veal shanks and brown on all sides, about 5 minutes per side.

Transfer the veal shanks to a 5-quart or larger crockery slow cooker. Surround with the onion, celery, carrot, garlic, and tomatoes. Mix the chicken broth and tomato paste together and pour over the veal and vegetables. Sprinkle with the basil and oregano.

Cover and cook on LOW for 8 to 10 hours. Meanwhile, make the garnish: Combine the parsley, lemon zest, and garlic. Set aside. Transfer the shanks to a heated serving platter. Sprinkle with half of the lemon-parsley mixture and keep warm.

Increase the cooking temperature of the cooker to HIGH and cook the pan juices, uncovered and stirring occasionally, until thick, about 15 minutes. Spoon the pan juices over the shanks and sprinkle with the remaining lemon-parsley mixture. Serve immediately.

○ PER SERVING: 12 g carbohydrate (includes 3 g dietary fiber), 51 g protein, 14 g fat, 386 calories
○ DIABETIC EXCHANGES: 2 vegetable, 7 lean meat, ½ fat

Orange-Parmesan Pork Roast with Root Vegetables

A slow cooker roasts this succulent pork loin dinner to perfection without heating up the kitchen. This is a surefire recipe for a no-fuss Sunday dinner, needing only a tossed green salad to complete the meal.

MAKES 6 SERVINGS

1 (3-pound) boneless pork loin
¹⁄₃ cup freshly grated Parmesan cheese
¹⁄₄ cup chopped fresh parsley
2 large cloves garlic, minced
1 tablespoon grated orange zest
1 tablespoon olive oil
6 small turnips, quartered
4 medium carrots, peeled and cut into 1-inch pieces

Using the tip of a sharp knife, cut 1-inch-long and ¼-inch-deep slits all over the surface of the roast. In a small bowl, combine the Parmesan cheese, parsley, garlic, and orange zest. Rub the mixture over the surface of the roast, making sure it gets into the slits.

Heat the oil in a large skillet over medium–high heat. Add the pork roast and brown on all sides. Place a metal rack or trivet in a 4½-quart or larger slow cooker. Place the roast on the rack. Arrange the vegetables around the roast.

Cover and cook on LOW 6 to 7 hours or until the center of the roast registers 165°F on an instant-read thermometer. Transfer the roast to a carving board and let stand for 10 minutes before thinly slicing. Serve with the vegetables and any pan juices.

○ PER SERVING: 8 g carbohydrate (includes 3 g fiber), 51 g protein, 13 g fat, 359 calories
○ DIABETIC EXCHANGES: 1¹⁄₂ vegetable, 6¹⁄₂ very lean meat

Pork Loin Stuffed with Dried Cherries

MAKES 6 SERVINGS

¹/₂ cup dried tart cherries

3 tablespoons boiling water

1 tablespoon cognac

1 tablespoon unsalted butter

1 bunch scallions, white part
   and 2 inches green, chopped

2 medium ribs celery, finely
   chopped

2 tablespoons chopped fresh
   parsley

¹/₂ teaspoon plus 1 tablespoon
   grated orange zest

¹/₂ teaspoon crushed dried
   thyme, divided

¹/₄ teaspoon crushed dried
   rosemary, divided

¹/₈ teaspoon ground allspice

1 (2-pound) boneless pork loin,
   trimmed of all fat and
   butterflied

Salt and freshly ground pepper,
   to taste

¹/₂ cup dry white wine

When my husband consulted to a company headquartered near the cherry-growing region of Michigan, I began to appreciate dried tart cherries, finding them a wonderful addition to all sorts of dishes from salads to desserts. Here I use them to stuff a pork loin roast. The result is festive enough for a company dinner.

In a small bowl, combine the cherries, boiling water, and cognac. Set aside to allow the cherries to soften.

In a large nonstick skillet, melt the butter over medium heat. Add the scallions and celery. Sauté until the vegetables are limp, about 5 minutes. Remove from the heat. Drain the cherries, reserving the liquid. Add the cherries to the skillet and stir in the parsley, ½ teaspoon orange zest, ¼ teaspoon of the thyme, ⅛ teaspoon of the rosemary, and the allspice. Mix well.

Lay the pork out flat on a work surface, fat side down. Spread the cherry mixture evenly over the pork. Roll up to enclose the stuffing and tie with kitchen string at 1½-inch intervals. Season the surface of the roast with salt, pepper, and the remaining thyme and rosemary. Place the roast, seam side down, in the bottom of a 5-quart or larger crockery slow cooker. Combine the wine and reserved cherry liquid. Pour over the roast.

Cover and cook on LOW 5 to 6 hours, until the center of the roast reaches 165°F on an instant-read thermometer. Transfer the roast to a carving board and keep warm. Pour the pan juices into a nonstick skillet. Skim off any surface fat. Bring the liquid to a boil and boil until reduced by one-third to thicken slightly. Carve the roast into ½-inch thick slices and nap each serving with the pan sauce.

○ PER SERVING: 9 g carbohydrate (includes 1 g dietary fiber), 31 g protein, 12 g fat, 278 calories

▪○ DIABETIC EXCHANGES: ½ fruit, 4½ lean meat, ½ fat

Italian Roast Pork with Fennel

This is a lovely roast for an autumn dinner or any special occasion. I'd serve this with a salad of radicchio and Boston lettuce, walnuts, and shavings of Asiago cheese with a lemon-garlic vinaigrette.

Trim the fennel, discarding the feathery tops and tough outer leaves. Slice each bulb vertically into 4 sections. Place in the bottom of a 5-quart or larger crockery slow cooker. Top with the onions.

Using a sharp knife, make deep incisions on the top of the pork roast. In a small bowl, mix together the garlic, rosemary, and oil. Rub the mixture over the roast, making sure some gets into the slits. Season the roast with salt and pepper and sprinkle with the Worcestershire sauce. Place the roast in the cooker and pour in the wine.

Cover and cook on LOW for 5 to 6 hours or on HIGH for 2 to 3 hours, until an instant-read thermometer inserted in the center of the roast registers 165°F. Transfer the roast to a carving board and keep warm.

Using a slotted spoon, transfer the fennel and onions to 6 heated dinner plates. Skim the fat from the surface of the cooking liquid. Transfer the cooking liquid to a saucepan and add the broth. Bring the mixture to a boil over medium-high heat and boil, stirring often, until slightly thickened, about 5 minutes. Remove from the heat and stir in the cream. Set aside.

Slice the pork into 6 chops and arrange on top of the fennel and onions. Pour some of the sauce over the top of each chop. Garnish each serving with a rosemary sprig and serve immediately.

MAKES 6 SERVINGS

3 large fennel bulbs

3 medium onions, thinly sliced crosswise

1 (3½- to 4-pound) rack of pork loin, chine bone removed and rack cracked between chops for easy carving

4 cloves garlic, minced

½ tablespoon finely chopped fresh rosemary plus 6 small sprigs, for garnish

1 tablespoon extra-virgin olive oil

Salt and freshly ground pepper, to taste

1 tablespoon Worcestershire sauce

¾ cup dry white wine

1 cup canned low-sodium chicken broth

¼ cup heavy cream

○ PER SERVING: 15 g carbohydrate (includes 5 g dietary fiber), 42 g protein, 31 g fat, 520 calories

○ DIABETIC EXCHANGES: 2 vegetable, 6 lean meat, ½ fat

Cuban Pork Roast with Citrus Mojo

MAKES 6 SERVINGS

1 (3-pound) boneless pork loin

2 teaspoons crushed dried
    oregano

1 teaspoon crushed dried thyme

1 teaspoon sweet paprika

4 cloves garlic, minced

2 tablespoons minced fresh
    cilantro

1 tablespoon olive oil

Citrus Mojo

½ cup extra-virgin olive oil,
    preferably Spanish

4 cloves garlic, peeled

¼ teaspoon crushed dried
    oregano

2 teaspoons fresh orange juice

1 teaspoon fresh lemon juice

1 teaspoon fresh lime juice

½ teaspoon freshly ground
    pepper

One of my favorite parts of Latino cuisine are the mojos—garlicky, olive oil–based dipping sauces that are used to intensify the flavors of most every food, meat, poultry, and fish. Here I've teamed traditional Cuban pork roasting seasonings with a citrus mojo. Latin cooks could use sour orange juice, but the combination of orange juice, lemon juice, and lime juice will suffice.

Using the tip of a sharp knife, cut 1-inch-long and ¼-inch-deep slits all over the surface of the roast. In a small bowl, combine the oregano, thyme, paprika, garlic, and cilantro. Rub the mixture over the surface of the roast, making sure it gets into the slits.

Heat the oil in a large skillet over medium–high heat. Add the roast and brown on all sides. Place a wire rack or trivet in the bottom of a 4½-quart or larger crockery slow cooker. Place the roast on the rack.

Cover and cook on LOW 6 to 7 hours, until an instant-read thermometer inserted into the center of the roast registers 170°F. Transfer the roast to a carving board and let stand for 10 minutes.

Meanwhile, to make the mojo: Combine all the ingredients in a food processor or blender. Process until smooth. Pour the mixture into 6 small bowls.

Carve the roast into thin slices. Arrange on heated dinner plates along with the bowls of mojo. Serve immediately.

○ **PER SERVING (PORK AND MOJO):** 1 g carbohydrate (includes trace dietary fiber), 45 g protein, 36 g fat, 524 calories
○ **DIABETIC EXCHANGES:** 6½ lean meat, 3½ fat
○ **PER SERVING (MOJO ONLY):** 1 g carbohydrate (includes trace dietary fiber), 0 protein, 17 g fat, 172 calories
○ **DIABETIC EXCHANGES:** 3½ fat

Jamaican Jerk Pork with Mango Relish

Jerk seasonings are showing up in supermarkets and restaurants, making it seem like a new food fad, but jerked meat has been around for centuries. Beef jerky is jerked (cured) meat, but to Jamaicans, jerk means the spice mixture that was once a preservative and is now a barbecue seasoning. Here, commercial jerk seasoning is rubbed onto pork tenderloin before slow cooking. The spicy-sweet relish is a perfect counterpoint to the hot zing of the jerked pork.

Rub the pork tenderloin with the jerk seasoning and sprinkle with the thyme. Place a wire rack or trivet in the bottom of a 5-quart or larger crockery slow cooker. Place the roast on the rack. Pour the water into the cooker.

Cover and cook on LOW for 8 to 10 hours or on HIGH for 4 to 5 hours. Transfer the pork to a carving board and let rest for 10 minutes before slicing and serving.

Meanwhile, to make the relish: Combine all the ingredients in a mixing bowl. Place in a small dish to serve with the pork.

O PER SERVING (PORK ONLY): 0 carbohydrate (includes 0 dietary fiber), 32 g protein, 7 g fat, 199 calories

O DIABETIC EXCHANGES: 5 lean meat

O PER SERVING (RELISH ONLY): 16 g carbohydrate (includes 1 g dietary fiber), trace protein, 1 g fat, 74 calories

O DIABETIC EXCHANGES: 1 fruit

MAKES 6 SERVINGS PLUS 1$\frac{1}{2}$ CUPS RELISH

1 (2-pound) boneless pork tenderloin, trimmed of fat

1 tablespoon Jamaican jerk seasoning

$\frac{1}{4}$ teaspoon crushed dried thyme

1 cup water

Mango Relish

1$\frac{1}{2}$ cups diced mango

2 tablespoons minced red bell pepper

3 scallions, white part and 1 inch green, finely minced

1 tablespoon minced fresh cilantro

1 teaspoon fresh lime juice

1 teaspoon canola oil

Gingered Pork with Vegetables

MAKES 6 SERVINGS

1 (2-pound) boneless pork tenderloin, trimmed of fat

1½ tablespoons canola oil, divided

2 medium carrots, peeled and sliced diagonally into ½-inch pieces

2 medium ribs celery, sliced diagonally into ½-inch pieces

1 bunch scallions, white part and 2 inches green, sliced thinly on the diagonal

2 cloves garlic, slivered

¼ cup reduced-sodium soy sauce

½ boiling water

1 instant beef bouillon cube (makes 2 cups broth)

2 tablespoons grated fresh ginger

⅛ teaspoon crushed red pepper flakes

1 (6-ounce) package sliced fresh mushrooms

Another time this dish could be made with chicken, beef, or lamb. The piquant sauce develops into a mahogany glaze as the dish slowly cooks.

Slice the tenderloin very thinly on the diagonal. Place in the bottom of a 3½-quart crockery slow cooker.

Heat 1 tablespoon of the canola oil in a large nonstick skillet over medium heat. Add the carrots, celery, scallions, and garlic. Sauté, tossing frequently, for 5 minutes. Spoon the vegetables over the pork. In a large measuring cup, combine the soy sauce, water, bouillon cube, ginger, and red pepper flakes. Pour into the cooker.

Cover and cook on LOW for 8 to 10 hours or on HIGH for 4 to 5 hours. Thirty minutes before the pork is done, heat the remaining ½ tablespoon oil in a nonstick sauté pan over medium–high heat. Add the mushrooms and sauté until the mushrooms are wilted and most of the liquid in the pan has evaporated, about 5 minutes. Transfer the mushrooms to the cooker. Cover and cook until the pork is cooked through.

To serve, arrange the pork slices on a heated serving platter. Top with the vegetables and pan sauce. Serve immediately.

○ PER SERVING: 6 g carbohydrate (includes 2 g dietary fiber), 35 g protein, 11 g fat, 263 calories

○ DIABETIC EXCHANGES: 1 vegetable, 5 lean meat, ½ fat

Polynesian Pork Roast with Sweet Potatoes

The tempting, exotic aromas from this Polynesian-inspired pork roast are sure to bring family members to the kitchen ahead of time. Put them to work making a tossed green salad and setting the table while you steam some fresh snow peas to finish the meal.

MAKES 6 SERVINGS

2 medium sweet potatoes, scrubbed and cut into 2-inch chunks

2 teaspoons canola oil

1 (2-pound) boneless pork loin roast

1 (6-ounce) can unsweetened crushed pineapple, drained

2 tablespoons reduced-sodium soy sauce

2 tablespoons fresh orange juice

2 tablespoons fresh lemon juice

2 cloves garlic, minced

2 tablespoons grated onion

1 tablespoon grated fresh ginger

1 serrano chile, seeded and minced

¼ teaspoon cayenne pepper

Place the sweet potatoes in the bottom of a 3½-quart or larger crockery slow cooker. In a large nonstick skillet, heat the oil over medium-high heat. Add the roast and brown on all sides, turning occasionally, about 10 minutes total. Transfer the roast to the slow cooker. Combine the remaining ingredients and pour over the roast.

Cover and cook on LOW for 8 to 10 hours or on HIGH for 4 to 5 hours. Transfer the roast to a carving board. Place the sweet potatoes at one end of a heated serving platter. If cooking on LOW, increase the cooking temperature to HIGH. Stir the pan juices and cook, uncovered, for 5 to 10 minutes to reduce slightly.

Carve the roast in thin slices and arrange on the serving platter. Spoon the pan juices over the pork and serve.

○ **PER SERVING:** 23 g carbohydrate (includes 2 g dietary fiber), 33 g protein, 12 g fat, 332 calories

○ **DIABETIC EXCHANGES:** 1 bread/starch, ½ fruit, 4½ lean meat, ½ fat

Pork Chops with Apples and Cabbage

MAKES 4 SERVINGS

1 small head red cabbage, quartered, cored, and cut into wedges

¼ cup diced onion

¼ cup diced carrot

¼ cup diced celery

1 clove garlic, minced

2 medium Granny Smith apples, peeled, cored, and diced

2 teaspoons extra-virgin olive oil

4 (about ¾-inch-thick) center-cut pork chops

¼ teaspoon crushed dried thyme

½ cup canned low-sodium chicken broth

¼ cup Calvados, apple brandy, or additional chicken broth

2 teaspoons Dijon mustard

This recipe's roots are from the Alsace region of France, where both Germany and France influence the cuisine. While the dish can be prepared with sauerkraut, I prefer the color and flavor of red cabbage.

Place the cabbage in a 4-quart or larger crockery slow cooker. Top with the onion, carrot, celery, garlic, and apples.

Heat the olive oil in a large skillet over medium-high heat. Add the pork chops and brown, turning once, about 2 minutes per side. Place the chops on top of the vegetables. In a measuring cup, combine the thyme, broth, Calvados, and mustard. Pour over the chops.

Cover and cook on LOW for 7 to 8 hours or on HIGH for 3½ to 4 hours. Transfer the pork chops to a plate. Pile the cabbage and apples on a heated serving platter and top with the chops. Serve immediately.

○ **PER SERVING:** 25 g carbohydrate (includes 6 g dietary fiber), 41 g protein, 14 g fat, 317 calories

○ **DIABETIC EXCHANGES:** ½ fruit, 2 vegetable, 3 lean meat, 1 fat

Pork Chops in Apricot-Kumquat Sauce

As the pork chops slowly cook, the flavors of the fruit melt into the pork. Use dried apricots from Turkey, if possible—their taste is far superior to domestic dried apricots.

Heat the oil in a large skillet over medium heat. Add the pork chops and brown, about 2 minutes per side. Set aside.

Cut the kumquats in half lengthwise and discard any seeds. Finely chopped the kumquats (including their skin) and combine with the apricots, ginger, onion, and garlic in the bottom of a 5-quart or larger crockery slow cooker. Top with the pork chops. In a glass measuring cup, combine the wine, tomato paste, and cardamom. Pour over the pork chops.

Cover and cook on LOW for 7 to 8 hours or on HIGH for 3½ to 4 hours. Transfer the chops to individual serving plates. Top with some of the fruit and pan sauce.

○ PER SERVING: 10 g carbohydrate (includes 2 g dietary fiber), 22 g protein, 12 g fat, 246 calories
○ DIABETIC EXCHANGES: ½ fruit, ½ vegetable, 3 lean meat, ½ fat

MAKES 6 SERVINGS

2 teaspoons extra-virgin olive oil
6 (about ¾-inch-thick) center-cut pork chops
4 fresh kumquats
6 dried apricots, cut into thin slivers
1 tablespoon grated fresh ginger
1 medium onion, chopped
1 clove garlic, minced
1 cup dry white wine
1 tablespoon tomato paste
¼ teaspoon ground cardamom

Pork Chops with Chipotle-Cranberry Sauce

MAKES 4 SERVINGS

4 (about ¾-inch-thick) center-cut pork chops

½ cup dried cranberries

1 medium onion, grated

1 clove garlic, minced

1 tablespoon finely chopped canned chipotle chiles in adobo sauce, or to taste

1 teaspoon finely minced fresh ginger

1 cup canned low-sodium chicken broth

2 teaspoons cornstarch, mixed with 1 tablespoon water

1 tablespoon chopped fresh cilantro

1 tablespoon snipped fresh chives

Dried cranberries will disintegrate during the long cooking time, but their flavor will be ever-present in the finished dish. You can temper or fire up the heat by the amount of chipotle chiles used.

Place the chops in the bottom of a 3½-quart or larger crockery slow cooker. Add the cranberries, onion, garlic, chipotle chiles, and ginger. Pour the broth into the cooker.

Cover and cook on LOW for 5 hours or on HIGH for 2½ hours, until the pork is tender. Transfer the chops to a heated serving platter and keep warm. Transfer the cooking liquid to a medium saucepan. Skim off any fat. Stir the cornstarch mixture and whisk into the cooking liquid. Cook over medium heat, stirring occasionally, until thickened and bubbly. Cook, stirring, for 2 minutes more. Stir in the cilantro and chives and spoon the sauce over the chops. Serve immediately.

○ **PER SERVING:** 18 g carbohydrate (includes 2 g dietary fiber), 30 g protein, 8 g fat, 214 calories

○ **DIABETIC EXCHANGES:** ½ fruit, 1 vegetable, 3 lean protein

Quick-and-Easy Pork Chops

Serve these savory chops with mashed turnips and a mixed green salad with sliced cucumbers, radishes, a sprinkle of blue cheese, and a purchased vinaigrette that has no more than 3 grams of carbohydrate per serving.

Spread each side of the pork chops with ½ teaspoon of the Dijon mustard. Season with salt and pepper. Place the onion in the bottom of a 3½-quart or larger crockery slow cooker. Arrange the pork chops on top of the onion. In a glass measuring cup, dissolve the bouillon cube in the boiling water. Stir in the wine and pour the mixture over the chops and sprinkle with the thyme.

Cover and cook on LOW for 5 to 6 hours or on HIGH for 2½ to 3 hours. Transfer the chops to a heated serving platter. Spoon the onion and pan juices over the chops. Serve immediately.

O **PER SERVING:** 6 g carbohydrate (includes 1 g dietary fiber), 23 g protein, 11 g fat, 216 calories

O **DIABETIC EXCHANGES:** ½ vegetable, 3 lean meat

MAKES 4 SERVINGS

4 (about ¾-inch-thick) center-cut pork chops

4 teaspoons Dijon mustard

Salt and freshly ground pepper, to taste

1 medium onion, sliced ½ inch thick

1 chicken bouillon cube (makes 2 cups broth)

¼ cup boiling water

¼ cup dry white wine

¼ teaspoon crushed dried thyme

Alpine Pork Ribs with Apples and Kraut

MAKES 4 SERVINGS

2 medium onions, thinly sliced
and separated into rings
2 cloves garlic, minced
1 (14½-ounce) can whole peeled
tomatoes, including juice
1 Granny Smith apple,
unpeeled, cored, and
chopped
1 (32-ounce) jar sauerkraut,
drained
2 pounds lean boneless
country-style pork ribs
1 cup low-carb light beer
¾ teaspoon caraway seed
1 teaspoon dry mustard
¼ teaspoon ground allspice

When my husband and I took our sons to Austria to ski, we stayed at the Europa Tyrol in Innsbruck, where a similar pork dish was offered on the nightly menu. Theirs was slow baked in the oven, but adapts superbly to a slow cooker.

Because we're all counting carbs, I've substituted low-carb light beer for the dark German beer that they used. The pork ribs come out fork-tender after the long, slow cooking. This dish is best when cooked on the LOW temperature setting.

Place the onions and garlic in the bottom of a 5-quart or larger crockery slow cooker. Drain the juice from the tomatoes and reserve. Coarsely chop the tomatoes and combine with the apple and sauerkraut. Spoon half of the mixture over the onion. Top with the pork ribs and spoon the remaining sauerkraut mixture over the pork.

In a small bowl, combine the reserved tomato juice, beer, caraway seed, dry mustard, and allspice. Pour evenly over the sauerkraut.

Cover and cook on LOW for 8 to 10 hours, until the pork is fork-tender. Transfer the pork and vegetables to a heated serving platter. Serve immediately.

○ PER SERVING: 23 g carbohydrate (includes 10 g dietary fiber), 43 g protein, 23 g fat, 485 calories
○ DIABETIC EXCHANGES: 4 vegetable, 5½ lean meat, 1 fat

Apricot-Mustard Glazed Ham

An all-time dinner buffet and picnic favorite, this ham provides end-less possibilities for leftovers.

MAKES 16 SERVINGS

1 (5-pound) fully cooked
    boneless ham
1/2 cup Dijon mustard
1/2 cup sugar-free apricot jam
Ground cloves, to taste
1 cup low-carb light beer

Place a wire rack in the bottom of a 5-quart or larger crockery slow cooker. Spread a layer of mustard on the top and sides of the ham. Top with a layer of the jam. Lightly sprinkle the ham with ground cloves. Place the ham on the rack in the slow cooker. Pour the beer into the cooker.

Cover and cook on HIGH for 1 hour. Reduce the temperature setting to LOW and cook for 6 to 7 hours. Transfer the ham to a carving board and let stand for 10 minutes before cutting into thin slices.

Transfer the pan juices to a small saucepan and skim off the fat from the surface. Bring the remaining mixture to a boil and cook, stirring frequently, until reduced to the consistency of a thin sauce. Pour the mixture into a gravy boat to spoon over the ham.

○ PER SERVING: 3 g carbohydrate (includes 0 dietary fiber), 40 g protein, 13 g fat, 267 calories
○ DIABETIC EXCHANGES: 4 1/2 lean meat

Leg of Lamb with Rosemary

MAKES 8 SERVINGS

1 clove garlic, minced

1 tablespoon grated fresh
   ginger

Salt and freshly ground pepper,
   to taste

1 (3-pound) boneless leg of
   lamb, trimmed of fat

1 large onion, coarsely chopped

¾ teaspoon dried rosemary
   leaves

1 (14-ounce) can low-sodium
   beef broth

1 tablespoon cornstarch,
   dissolved in 1 tablespoon
   water

2 tablespoons ketchup

2 tablespoons reduced-sodium
   soy sauce

½ teaspoon grated lemon zest

*This recipe comes from Jerry Langston, the wife of a friend of my hus-
band from university days. The flavorful gravy is delicious spooned
over the sliced lamb.*

Combine the garlic, ginger, salt, and pepper. Rub over the lamb.
Place a wire rack or trivet in the bottom of a 5-quart or larger
crockery slow cooker. Place the lamb on the rack. Add the
onion and rosemary to the cooker. Pour in the broth.

Cover and cook on LOW for 8 to 10 hours or on HIGH
for 4 to 5 hours. Baste the lamb generously with the broth and
transfer to a carving board. Keep warm.

Pour the pan juices through a wire strainer, pressing the
onion with the back of a wooden spoon to force as much solids
as possible through the strainer. Discard the onion solids. Skim
the fat from the pan juices and return to the cooker.

If cooking on LOW, increase the temperature setting to
HIGH. In a small bowl, whisk together the dissolved cornstarch, ketchup, soy sauce, and lemon zest. Whisk the mixture
into the pan juices and cook, uncovered, stirring occasionally,
until thickened into a thin gravy.

Carve the lamb and place the gravy in a sauceboat. Pass the
gravy separately to pour over the lamb.

○ **PER SERVING:** 4 g carbohydrate (includes trace dietary fiber), 32 g
    protein, 9 g fat, 227 calories
○ **DIABETIC EXCHANGES:** ½ vegetable, 4½ lean meat

Lamb Shanks with Tomatoes and White Beans

Very popular in French country cooking, thrifty lamb shanks braised with tomatoes and white beans become a full-flavored meal. I've added serrano chiles to my recipe—just enough heat to tease the palate. This recipe should only be cooked on the LOW setting.

MAKES 4 SERVINGS

4 (about 1 pound total) lamb shanks

Salt and freshly ground pepper, to taste

1 tablespoon extra-virgin olive oil

1 small onion, minced

4 cloves garlic, minced

1 cup full-bodied red wine, such as Shiraz

1 (28-ounce) can whole plum tomatoes, including juice

1 (14-ounce) can low-sodium chicken broth

3 sprigs fresh rosemary

1 (15-ounce) can white beans, rinsed and drained

Season the lamb shanks with salt and pepper. Heat the olive oil in a large nonstick skillet over medium-high heat. Add the lamb shanks and brown, about 5 minutes per side.

Meanwhile, put the onion in the bottom of a 5-quart or larger crockery slow cooker. Transfer the lamb shanks to the cooker. Add the garlic and wine to the skillet and cook, scraping the bottom of the skillet with a wooden spoon to loosen any browned bits, for 2 minutes. Pour the wine mixture over the lamb shanks. Add the tomatoes with the juice, broth, and rosemary.

Cover and cook on LOW for 8 to 9 hours. Thirty minutes before the cooking time is complete, stir the beans into the pan juices. Cover and cook until the lamb shanks are tender and the beans are heated through.

To serve, place each lamb shank in a warm shallow bowl; ladle some of the sauce, beans, and vegetables around each shank, discarding the rosemary sprigs. Serve immediately.

○ PER SERVING: 29 g carbohydrate (includes 7 g dietary fiber), 60 g protein, 14 g fat, 453 calories

○ DIABETIC EXCHANGES: 1 bread/starch, 2 vegetable, 7 lean meat, ½ fat

Go-Withs:
Vegetable Side Dishes

TO MY WAY of thinking, vegetables are best cooked on top of the stove, in the microwave, or grilled. There are some exceptions where the slow cooker does a better job—with artichokes, onions, and garlic. It also makes cooking ratatouille a snap. These alone make owning a slow cooker worthwhile. If you like the smoky flavor of slow-cooked green beans and slow-baked tomatoes, give My Mom's Green Beans a try as well. I've also included a recipe for a "mystery" vegetable, which I've served several times with everyone at the table thinking it's high-carb potatoes when it's actually low-carb turnips. Finally, there's a scrumptious recipe with wild rice, dried cherries, and pecans that's worthy of your most special dinner, including the big feast at Thanksgiving, Christmas, or Easter.

My Mom's Green Beans

When I was growing up in Kansas, we grew lots of vegetables on our suburban ranch. Once we owned a freezer, my mother would freeze bushels of green beans. This dish showed up at our dinner table quite regularly, either simmered on top of the stove for an hour or more or cooked in a pressure cooker. When she was given a Crock-Pot® slow cooker, the cooking process was simplified. Cooked this way, the beans are no longer the bright emerald color of crisp-cooked green beans, but the flavor is smoky and wonderful.

Combine all of the ingredients in a 3½-quart or larger crockery slow cooker. Cover and cook on LOW for about 5 hours, until the beans are very tender. Taste and season with salt and pepper as needed.

Transfer to a heated serving dish and serve immediately.

O **PER SERVING:** 14 g carbohydrate (includes 3 g dietary fiber), 5 protein, 2 g fat, 87 calories
O **DIABETIC EXCHANGE:** 2 vegetable, ½ lean meat

MAKES 8 SERVINGS

4 (1-ounce) slices lean ham, diced

1 medium onion, chopped

1½ pounds fresh green beans, trimmed and cut into 1-inch lengths

1 (14½-ounce) can stewed tomatoes, including juice

¾ cup water

1 tablespoon cider vinegar

1 tablespoon packed light brown sugar

Salt and freshly ground pepper, to taste

Stuffed Artichokes

MAKES 4 SERVINGS

4 large globe artichokes

2 tablespoons plus 2 teaspoons fresh lemon juice

2 slices whole wheat bread

1 medium onion, finely chopped

1 clove garlic, minced

⅓ cup finely chopped fresh parsley

2 plum tomatoes, seeded and finely chopped

2 teaspoons capers, rinsed and chopped

Salt and freshly ground pepper, to taste

1 tablespoon extra-virgin olive oil

2 cups dry white wine or water

¼ cup (½ stick) unsalted butter

2 teaspoons fresh lemon juice

When we lived in Southern California, I tried several combinations of plantings around the pool. When most everything suffered from the chemicals of the water splashed from the pool by my sons and their many friends, I called my neighbor's father, who was the dean of agriculture at U.C. Davis. He suggested planting artichokes. They were impervious to the pool water and thrived in the constant hot sun. It was during that time that I started serving artichokes frequently as a first course for special dinners or as the entrée for a light lunch. This recipe is a winner, and so easy in a slow cooker.

Wash the artichokes under cold running water. Pull off the small leaves and cut the stem off at the base. Slice off the top quarter of each artichoke and, if desired, trim off the thorny tips of each leaf. Stand the artichokes upright and spread the leaves with your fingers to expose the pale green inner cone of leaves. Using a small spoon, scoop out and discard this cone and the fuzzy choke underneath. Place the artichokes in a large bowl of cold water that has been mixed with the 2 tablespoons lemon juice. Set aside.

Meanwhile, make fresh bread crumbs of the whole wheat bread and mix with the onion, garlic, parsley, tomatoes, capers, salt, and pepper. Drain the artichokes and stuff the centers with the bread crumb mixture. Stand the artichokes up in a 5-quart or larger crockery slow cooker. Drizzle with the olive oil and pour the wine around the artichokes.

Cover and cook on HIGH for 4 hours, until a leaf can be easily pulled from an artichoke. When the artichokes are done, melt the butter in a small nonstick skillet over low heat. Cook, stirring, for 3 to 5 minutes, until the butter begins to brown. Do not burn. Remove from heat and stir in the 2 teaspoons lemon juice. Place each artichoke on a heated serving plate and drizzle 1 tablespoon of the lemon butter over the top. Serve immediately.

○ **PER SERVING:** 28 g carbohydrate (includes 11 g dietary fiber), 8 g protein, 16 g fat, 272 calories

○ **DIABETIC EXCHANGES:** 4 vegetable, 3 fat

Caramelized Garlic

Slow cooking tames the bite of garlic, giving it a mellow sweetness with a jamlike consistency. I keep this garlic on hand to smear onto grilled meat or vegetables and to use in recipes whenever roasted garlic is called for, such as for the delectable Garlic Flan (page 166) or Caramelized Garlic Soup (page 39).

MAKES ABOUT 20 CLOVES PLUS ¹/₃ CUP GARLIC OIL

2 heads garlic
¹/₃ cup extra-virgin olive oil
Salt and freshly ground pepper,
    to taste

Remove the papery exterior from the heads of garlic, but do not separate or peel the cloves. Using a serrated knife, cut a ¼-inch slice off the top of the heads to expose just the tops of the cloves. Place the garlic heads in the bottom of a 1-quart crockery slow cooker. Pour the olive oil over the garlic. Sprinkle with salt and pepper.

Cover and cook on HIGH for 4 to 6 hours, until the garlic is very soft when pierced with the tip of a sharp knife. Cool the garlic in the oil.

Squeeze the garlic purée from the cloves and discard the peels. Use the garlic as suggested in the headnote above or refrigerate in a covered container for up to 3 days. Refrigerate the garlic-flavored olive oil to use in cooking or in making salad dressing.

○ **PER 2-CLOVE SERVING:** 9 g carbohydrate (includes <1 g dietary fiber), 2 g protein, 78 calories
○ **DIABETIC EXCHANGES:** 1 fat

Garlic Flan

MAKES 4 SERVINGS

1 cup heavy cream

2 large eggs

1 large egg yolk

1/2 cup caramelized garlic purée
   (see page 165)

1/4 cup freshly grated Parmesan
   cheese

Salt and freshly ground pepper,
   to taste

Butter for the custard cups

You can serve this savory flan as a vegetable accompaniment to grilled or roasted meats, seafood, or poultry. You can also serve it as a first course. At Café Terra Cotta in Tucson, Arizona, chef/owner Donna Nordin drizzles garlic flan with jalapeño chile–spiked vinaigrette and sprinkles it with toasted hazelnuts. Nordin also adds a finely minced jalapeño chile to the custard mixture, but I prefer my version, which uses a bit of grated Parmesan cheese.

In a medium saucepan, heat the cream over medium heat until hot. Remove from the heat and allow to cool slightly.

In a bowl, beat together the eggs and egg yolk. Add 1/4 cup of the hot cream to the eggs, whisking thoroughly. Stir in the remaining hot cream, garlic purée, and Parmesan cheese. Butter 4 (4-ounce) custard cups. Divide the custard mixture among the prepared cups.

Place a wire rack or trivet in the bottom of a 5-quart or larger crockery slow cooker. Cover each cup with a small piece of aluminum foil. Position the filled custard cups on top of the trivet. Pour 2 cups boiling water around the cups.

Cover and cook on HIGH 1¼ to 1¾ hours, until the custards are just set. Allow to cool slightly before running a knife around the inside of the custard cups. Unmold onto serving plates. Serve warm.

O PER SERVING: 10 g carbohydrate (includes <1 g dietary fiber), 8 g protein, 27 g fat, 312 calories

O DIABETIC EXCHANGES: 1 lean meat, 5 fat

Sweet Onion Confit

If your market doesn't carry Vidalia onions, use Texas 1015, Walla Walla, or Maui onions. Don't try this with a Spanish or white onion, as you won't get a sweet, mahogany-colored confit.

Place all the ingredients in a 4-quart or larger crockery slow cooker. Cover and cook on LOW for 12 to 14 hours, until the onions are very tender and a deep brown in color. Taste and add salt and pepper as needed. Serve, or transfer to a container and refrigerate for up to 3 days.

○ PER SERVING: 7 g carbohydrate (includes 2 g dietary fiber), 2 g protein, 4 g fat, 72 calories
○ DIABETIC EXCHANGES: 1½ vegetable, ½ fat

MAKES ABOUT 3½ CUPS; 12 SERVINGS

3 pounds Vidalia or other sweet onions, thinly sliced

4 tablespoons (½ stick) unsalted butter

¼ cup dry white wine or canned low-sodium chicken broth

Salt and freshly ground pepper, to taste

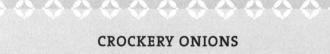

CROCKERY ONIONS

These onions are ideal, hot or lukewarm, with grilled meat and chicken or as an addition to any number of recipes. I've given you recipes using Vidalia or other sweet onions, as well as red onions. Both are luscious, and caramelizing them in a slow cooker eliminates the possibility of burning that exists when you cook them on top of the stove.

Red Onion Confit

MAKES ABOUT 3½ CUPS;
12 SERVINGS

3 pounds red onions, thinly
  sliced
4 tablespoons (½ stick)
  unsalted butter
1 tablespoon light brown sugar
¼ cup full-bodied dry red wine
1 teaspoon red wine vinegar, or
  more to taste
Salt and freshly ground pepper,
  to taste

Some trendy chefs now offer this delicious confit packed in jars with their private food label. It's super easy to make in your slow cooker.

Place the onions, butter, brown sugar, and wine in a 4-quart or larger crockery slow cooker. Cover and cook on LOW for 12 to 14 hours, until the onions are very tender and deeply colored. Stir in the vinegar and season with salt and pepper. Serve or transfer to a container and refrigerate for up to 3 days.

○ PER SERVING: 9 g carbohydrate (includes 2 g dietary fiber), 2 g protein, 4 g fat, 77 calories
○ DIABETIC EXCHANGES: 1½ vegetable, ½ fat

Slow-Cooked Ratatouille

By cooking this Provençal classic in a slow cooker, you eliminate all possibility of scorching as the vegetable juices cook down to a glaze. The dish lasts for several days in the refrigerator, so make plenty. It's wonderful hot or served at room temperature on a summer day.

Place the eggplants and zucchini in a large colander and lightly sprinkle with salt. Toss lightly. Let stand until the vegetables release their juices, about 30 minutes. Pat dry with paper towels.

Heat 1 tablespoon of the olive oil in a large nonstick skillet over medium heat. Add the eggplants and zucchini in 2 batches and sauté until lightly browned, stirring often, about 5 minutes per batch. Using a slotted spoon, transfer the mixture to a 5-quart or larger crockery slow cooker. Add the remaining olive oil to the skillet and sauté the onions, garlic, and bell peppers until soft, about 4 minutes. Using a slotted spoon, transfer these vegetables to the slow cooker. Stir in the remaining ingredients *except* the basil.

Cover and cook on LOW for 6 to 7 hours, until the vegetables are very tender. If the ratatouille has excess liquid, uncover, and increase the cooking temperature to HIGH. Cook, stirring occasionally, for 15 to 20 minutes, until thickened. Stir in the basil. Serve hot or at room temperature.

○ PER SERVING: 21 g carbohydrate (includes 5 g dietary fiber), 3 g protein, 3 g fat, 109 calories
○ DIABETIC EXCHANGES: 3 vegetable, ½ fat

MAKES 12 SERVINGS

2 medium eggplants (about 2½ pounds total), unpeeled and cut into 1-inch cubes
4 medium zucchini, quartered lengthwise and cut into 1-inch chunks
Salt
2 tablespoons extra-virgin olive oil, divided
2 medium onions, chopped
4 cloves garlic, minced
2 large red bell peppers, cut into 1-inch squares
2 medium yellow squash, cut in half lengthwise and cut into ½-inch slices
2 (28-ounce) cans peeled plum tomatoes, including juice
2 tablespoons tomato paste
2 teaspoons *herbes de Provence* (see page 67)
Freshly ground pepper, to taste
½ cup chopped fresh basil

Crockery Tomato Casserole

MAKES 6 SERVINGS

6 large plum tomatoes, halved lengthwise

4 cloves garlic, minced

1 jalapeño chile, seeded and minced (optional)

¼ cup extra-virgin olive oil

2 tablespoons fresh lemon juice

Salt and freshly ground pepper, to taste

2 tablespoons snipped fresh chives (optional)

Growing up in Kansas where my mom's pantry shelf was lined with home-canned tomatoes, we frequently had a tomato casserole on nights when my mom made meat loaf or baked chicken. I ran across her recipe recently and, upon trying it, found the tomatoes to be watery and lacking in flavor. I started experimenting with fresh tomatoes and my slow cooker and came up with this tasty alternative. You can jazz it up further with the addition of the optional jalapeño chile.

Put the tomatoes, cut sides up, in a 5-quart or larger crockery slow cooker. Sprinkle with the garlic and chile, if using. Drizzle with the olive oil and lemon juice. Season with salt and pepper.

Cover and cook on LOW for 6 to 8 hours, until the tomatoes are reduced in size but still retain their shape. Transfer the tomatoes and pan juices to a heated serving dish and, if using, sprinkle with the chives.

○ **PER SERVING:** 4 g carbohydrate (includes 1 g dietary fiber), 1 g protein, 9 g fat, 99 calories

○ **DIABETIC EXCHANGES:** ½ vegetable, 2 fat

Slow-Roasted Vegetables

Slow roasting is a cooking technique as old as our country. Native Americans were seen roasting vegetables buried under thick layers of grass by the early explorers, and pioneer housewives roasted vegetables in the kitchen hearth, buried under a thick layer of ashes. The slow cooker roasts vegetables to perfection.

Japanese eggplants are long, thin, pale purple, and don't require salting. If your supermarket doesn't carry them, try an Asian market. Small Italian eggplants can be used instead with good results.

Cut the squash in half and remove the seeds. Cut the squash into 2-inch wedges and place in the bottom of a 3½-quart or larger crockery slow cooker. Add the remaining vegetables and drizzle with the olive oil. Sprinkle with the thyme, red pepper flakes, salt, and pepper.

Cover and cook on LOW for 7 to 8 hours, until the vegetables are tender. Arrange the vegetables on a large, heated serving platter. Sprinkle with the cheese and scatter the basil on top. Serve immediately.

○ PER SERVING: 9 g carbohydrate (includes 2 g dietary fiber), 3 g protein, 3 g fat, 73 calories

○ DIABETIC EXCHANGES: 1½ vegetable, ½ fat

MAKES 12 SERVINGS

1 (about 1-pound) Sweet Dumpling or acorn squash

12 whole baby carrots, peeled

3 baby Japanese eggplants, unpeeled and halved lengthwise

12 small pearl onions, peeled (see page 58)

6 plum tomatoes, cut in half lengthwise

2 tablespoons extra-virgin olive oil

1 teaspoon crushed dried thyme

¼ teaspoon crushed red pepper flakes

Salt and freshly ground pepper, to taste

½ cup freshly grated Parmesan cheese

¼ cup coarsely chopped fresh basil

Mystery Vegetable

MAKES 8 SERVINGS

Unsalted butter for greasing the slow cooker

2½ pounds medium white turnips, very thinly sliced

1 small red onion, cut in half and thinly sliced

3 cloves garlic, minced

Salt and freshly ground pepper, to taste

6 ounces cream cheese, cut into 1-inch cubes

6 tablespoons shredded fontina cheese

If you don't tell them, most everyone at your table won't be able to guess what this is—maybe potatoes, but certainly not turnips. These are meltingly delicious.

This recipe is best cooked on the HIGH setting.

Butter a 3½-quart or larger crockery slow cooker. Arrange one-third of the turnip slices in the cooker. Top with one-third of the onion slices and one-third of the garlic. Lightly sprinkle with salt and pepper. Scatter one-third of the cream cheese and 2 tablespoons of the fontina cheese over the top. Repeat the layers twice, ending with the cream cheese and fontina cheese.

Cover and cook on HIGH for 2 to 2½ hours, until the turnips are very tender. Serve hot.

○ **PER SERVING:** 8 g carbohydrate (includes 3 g dietary fiber), 3 g protein, 8 g fat, 111 calories

○ **DIABETIC EXCHANGES:** 1½ vegetable, 1½ fat

Wild Rice Casserole with Cherries and Pecans

Nutty-flavored wild rice combines with dried cherries for a spectacular dish that's relatively low in carbs for a grain. Remember this when you're pulling out all the stops for a special dinner for family or friends.

In a large nonstick skillet, melt the butter over medium heat. Add the shallots and celery and sauté until the vegetables are limp, about 4 minutes. Transfer the mixture to a 3½-quart or larger crockery slow cooker. Stir in the broth, wild rice, thyme, salt, and pepper.

Cover and cook on HIGH for 4 to 5 hours, until the rice is almost tender. Meanwhile, heat the cherries and cognac in a small saucepan on top of the stove until the mixture comes to a boil. Remove and set aside for the cherries to soften.

Stir the cherry mixture into the rice. Re-cover and cook until the rice is tender, 15 to 30 minutes. Transfer the rice to a serving dish and sprinkle with the pecans. Serve hot.

○ PER SERVING: 19 g carbohydrate (includes 2 g dietary fiber), 4 g protein, 5 g fat, 142 calories

○ DIABETIC EXCHANGES: 1 bread/starch, ½ vegetable, 1 fat

MAKES 16 SERVINGS

2 tablespoons unsalted butter

4 shallots, finely minced

2 medium celery ribs, chopped

4 cups canned low-sodium chicken broth

2 cups wild rice, rinsed and drained

½ teaspoon crushed dried thyme

½ teaspoon salt

½ teaspoon freshly ground pepper

⅓ cup dried cherries

¼ cup cognac or orange juice

½ cup coarsely chopped pecans, toasted

Delectable Desserts

THESE WERE THE MOST difficult recipes to develop. To be sure, a slow cooker can make a fabulous steamed cranberry pudding, a scrumptious cheesecake, a tasty fruit cobbler with pastry topping, a molded gingerbread, or a decadent chocolate bread pudding. When you can use sugar and flour, it's easy, and the slow cooker does a superb job. But when you must take out the carbs contained in sugar and flour, you don't have much left with which to work—poached or slow-cooked fruit, creamy custard, and little more.

The few dessert recipes that I do offer are all terrific, so try them for even your most elegant of dinners: Apples Slow-Cooked in Port, an All-Day Chunky Applesauce that has many uses, Rustic Apple Brown Betty, Baked Orange Custards that can easily be turned into Orange Crème Brûlée, Slow-Poached Pears in Wine with a Chocolate Drizzle, and Slow-Baked Fruit.

Apples Slow-Cooked in Port

Here's an old favorite, made in a slow cooker without sugar. Pears can be baked in the same manner for an easy, comforting dessert.

Using a small paring knife, core and peel the apples halfway down from the stem end. Place in the bottom of a 3½-quart or larger slow cooker. Sprinkle with the brown sugar substitute, cinnamon, and nutmeg. Pour the port and water over the apples and sprinkle with the lemon zest.

Cover and cook on LOW for 3 to 4 hours. Transfer the apples to individual dessert dishes and sprinkle each serving with ½ tablespoon of the walnuts. Pour the pan juices into a small saucepan and place on top of the stove over medium-high heat. Cook, uncovered, until reduced by half. Spoon the juices over each apple and serve hot with sour cream or softly whipped cream, if desired.

O **PER SERVING (APPLE ONLY):** 19 g carbohydrate (includes 2 g dietary fiber, 1 g protein, 3 g fat

O **DIABETIC EXCHANGES:** 1 fruit, ½ fat

MAKES 6 SERVINGS

6 small cooking apples, such as Jonathan or Rome Beauty (about 1 pound total)

3 tablespoons spoonable brown sugar substitute

Ground cinnamon, to taste

Dash ground nutmeg

⅓ cup port wine

¼ cup water

1 tablespoon grated lemon zest

3 tablespoons chopped walnuts

Sour cream or whipped cream for topping (optional)

Rustic Apple Brown Betty

MAKES 4 SERVINGS

4 medium cooking apples, such
   as Jonathan or Rome Beauty,
   peeled, cored, and each cut
   into 8 wedges
2 slices whole wheat bread,
   torn into pieces
4 tablespoons unsalted butter,
   melted
3 tablespoons spoonable brown
   sugar substitute
1 teaspoon ground cinnamon
¼ teaspoon ground allspice
¼ cup coarsely chopped
   walnuts, toasted
Whipped cream (optional)

*Apples are a satisfying dessert, especially when made in this manner.
If you like, serve this with a drift of whipped cream.*

Place the apples in the bottom of a 3½-quart crockery slow
cooker. Pulse the bread in a food processor to form fine bread
crumbs. Transfer to a small bowl and stir in the remaining ingredients *except* the walnuts and whipped cream, if using. Sprinkle the crumb mixture over the apples.

Cover and cook on LOW for 3 to 4 hours or on HIGH for
2 hours. Spoon the apples into individual serving bowls and
sprinkle with the walnuts. Garnish each serving with a dollop
of whipped cream, if using. Serve hot or warm.

○ PER SERVING (BETTY ONLY): 20 g carbohydrate (includes 3 g dietary
   fiber), 2 g protein, 8 g fat, 145 calories
○ DIABETIC EXCHANGES: ½ bread/starch, 1 fruit, 1½ fat

A SAUCE OF MANY USES

Applesauce is not just for dessert.

- Serve applesauce as an accompaniment to pork roast,
  baked ham, or roasted duck or chicken.

- Use as a light spread for your morning whole-grain
  low-carb toast.

- Stir applesauce into plain low-fat yogurt for a nutri-
  tious snack.

- Fold it into crème fraîche or whipped cream for a
  simple dessert.

- Make an elegant dessert by placing a scoop of low-
  carb ice cream in a stemmed glass. Top with ½ cup
  applesauce and crumble an amaretti cookie or two
  (the tiny ones in the Italian red tin) on top.

All-Day Chunky Applesauce

A trek to apple country has been a fall tradition at my house, whether we were living on the West Coast, East Coast, or here in Texas. At the farmstands of each orchard, one could watch the farmers press apples for cider, whip up huge kettles of apple butter, or cook large vats of applesauce. It was at one of these stands that I discovered that the best applesauce is sweetened naturally with apple cider, not sugar. Using a slow cooker eliminates the possibility of scorching the apples as they are cooked until broken down and saucy.

MAKES ABOUT 8 CUPS; 24 SERVINGS

6 pounds apples, preferably McIntosh, Jonathan, or Cortland, peeled, cored, and quartered
1 cup apple cider
1 (3-inch) cinnamon stick
½ teaspoon ground cardamom
2 tablespoons fresh lemon juice
2 tablespoons unsalted butter

Place all ingredients *except* the butter in the bottom of a 3½-quart or larger crockery slow cooker.

Cover and cook on LOW for 6 to 8 hours or on HIGH for 3 to 4 hours, until the apples are very tender and saucy.

Remove and discard the cinnamon stick. Using a wooden spoon, stir in the butter, mashing any large chunks with the back of the spoon to your desired consistency. See page 176 for serving suggestions. Refrigerate leftover applesauce in a sealed container; use within 5 days.

○ PER ⅓-CUP SERVING: 18 g carbohydrate (includes 4 g dietary fiber), trace protein, <1 g fat, 73 calories
○ DIABETIC EXCHANGES: 1 fruit

Baked Orange Custards

MAKES 4 SERVINGS

1¼ cups heavy cream

1¼ cups whole milk

Grated zest from 2 medium
    oranges

1 (3-inch) cinnamon stick

Pinch salt

¼ cup Splenda sugar substitute

1 tablespoon Grand Marnier or
    other orange liqueur
    (optional)

½ teaspoon pure vanilla
    extract

4 large egg yolks, at room
    temperature

2 cups boiling water

A great dessert most any time of the year; it's not too sweet but deliciously filling. For special occasions, the simple custard can easily be turned into Orange Crème Brûlée (see page 179).

Combine the cream, milk, orange zest, cinnamon stick, and salt in a medium saucepan. Bring to a boil; remove from heat and allow to stand, covered, for 10 minutes. Discard the cinnamon stick. Whisk in the salt, Splenda, Grand Marnier (if using), and vanilla.

In a medium bowl, whisk the egg yolks and, while whisking, very slowly add the hot cream mixture. Strain the mixture into 4 (6-ounce) custard cups. Place a trivet in the bottom of a 5-quart or larger crockery slow cooker. Position the filled custard cups on top of the trivet. Cover each cup with a small piece of aluminum foil. Pour 2 cups boiling water around the cups.

Cover and cook on HIGH until a knife inserted in the center of a custard comes out clean, 1¼ to 1¾ hours. Uncover and let the custard cups stand in the cooker until cool enough to remove. Refrigerate, covered, until firm, at least 3 hours or overnight.

○ **PER SERVING:** 8 g carbohydrate (includes trace dietary fiber), 7 g protein, 35 g fat, 371 calories

○ **DIABETIC EXCHANGES:** ½ skim milk, ½ very lean meat, 7 fat

VARIATION

Orange Crème Brûlée

Evenly sprinkle each custard with ½ teaspoon brown sugar. Use a special kitchen blowtorch to caramelize the top, or set the cups under a hot broiler, about 4 inches from the source of heat, and broil until the tops are brown and bubbly, about 2 minutes. Let sit several minutes until the sugar hardens and cools before serving.

- O **PER SERVING:** 13 g carbohydrate (includes trace dietary fiber), 7 g protein, 35 g fat, 388 calories
- O **DIABETIC EXCHANGES:** ½ skim milk, ½ very lean meat, 7 fat

FRESH FRUIT

Most of the time, I opt for a piece of fresh fruit for dessert, perhaps with a drift of crème fraîche or whipped cream. Even with fresh fruit, you must know the portion size or you can easily exceed your carb limit. Here are the carb contents of the most popular fresh fruits:

½ of a medium apple, with skin (11 grams of carbohydrate)

4 apricots (16 grams of carbohydrate)

¾ cup blueberries (15 grams of carbohydrate)

1 cup cubed cantaloupe (13 grams of carbohydrate)

1 medium carambola or star fruit (15 grams of carbohydrate)

13 sweet cherries (15 grams of carbohydrate)

1 large fig (12 grams of carbohydrate)

½ large grapefruit (13 grams of carbohydrate)

17 seedless grapes (15 grams of carbohydrate)

1 cup honeydew melon cubes (16 grams of carbohydrate)

1 large kiwifruit (14 grams of carbohydrate)

½ cup sliced mango (14 grams of carbohydrate)

1 large nectarine (16 grams of carbohydrate)

1 large orange (15 grams of carbohydrate)

1 cup papaya cubes (14 grams of carbohydrate)

1 large peach (17 grams of carbohydrate)

½ of a large pear with skin (16 grams of carbohydrate)

¾ cup cubed pineapple (14 grams of carbohydrate)

2 medium plums (17 grams of carbohydrate)

1 cup raspberries (14 grams of carbohydrate)

1½ cups whole strawberries (15 grams of carbohydrate)

2 medium tangerines (19 grams of carbohydrate)

1¼ cups watermelon cubes (14 grams of carbohydrate)

NOTE:

Bananas are very high in carbohydrates and are usually not recommended for low-carb diets. If you are craving a banana, have it with breakfast when your body can best handle the rise in blood sugar levels. Even then, half of a medium banana will cost you 15 grams of carbohydrate.

Slow-Poached Pears with a Chocolate Drizzle

MAKES 4 SERVINGS

2 cups dry white wine, or more as needed to cover the pears
2 tablespoons fresh lemon juice
¼ cup Splenda sugar substitute
1 (2-inch) cinnamon stick
4 whole cloves
2 (4-inch) strip orange zest
1 (4-inch) strip lemon zest
2 ripe but firm medium Bartlett pears
¼ cups semisweet chocolate chips

Pears poached in wine are a classic dessert and don't cost that many carbs. They are great served hot or cold, but for special occasions, you might want to serve them warm with a drizzle of chocolate for a knife-and-fork dessert.

This recipe works best in a 3½-quart crockery slow cooker to ensure that the pears are submerged in the wine.

Place all the ingredients *except* the pears and chocolate chips in a 3½-quart crockery slow cooker. Stir, cover, and cook on HIGH until the mixture is hot and the Splenda has dissolved, 20 to 30 minutes. Meanwhile, peel the pears. Cut in half lengthwise and remove the cores. Place the pears in the slow cooker, cut-side down, adding additional wine as needed to cover the pears.

Cover and cook on LOW for 3 to 4 hours or on HIGH for 1½ to 2 hours, basting occasionally, just until tender. Transfer the pears to a shallow dish, cut-side up. Cool, basting occasionally, with the poaching liquid.

When ready to serve, transfer the pears, cut-sides up, to individual dessert dishes. Spoon some of the poaching liquid over each pear.

Place the chocolate chips in a glass measuring cup and microwave at 70 percent power, stirring every 20 seconds, until the chocolate is melted and smooth. Drizzle over the pears in a random pattern and serve.

○ **PER SERVING:** 22 g carbohydrate (includes 3 g dietary fiber), 1 g protein, 4 g fat, 119 calories
○ **DIABETIC EXCHANGES:** 1 fruit, ½ fat

Slow-Baked Fruit

A medley of fresh fruits is gently slow-poached for this colorful dessert. Serve it warm or chilled for a low-carb alternative to high-carb cookies and cake.

In a 3½-quart crockery slow cooker, combine all the ingredients except the crème fraîche, if using. Cover and cook on LOW for 5 to 6 hours or on HIGH for 2½ to 3 hours. Cool slightly or chill before serving. Spoon into bowls. If using, dollop each serving with crème fraîche.

○ PER SERVING (FRUIT ONLY): 17 g carbohydrate (includes 1 g dietary fiber), 1 g protein, 0 fat, 71 calories

○ DIABETIC EXCHANGES: 1 fruit

MAKES 8 SERVINGS

½ cup water

3 tablespoons Splenda sugar substitute

1 tablespoon fresh lemon juice

1 tablespoon grated lemon zest

6 cups mixed seasonal fruit, such as cut-up plums, peaches, apricots, apples, pears, pitted cherries, or seedless grapes

Crème fraîche (optional)

Metric Conversion Charts

Comparison to Metric Measure				
When You Know	**Symbol**	**Multiply By**	**To Find**	**Symbol**
teaspoons	tsp	5.0	milliliter	ml
tablespoons	tbsp	15.0f	milliliters	ml
fluid ounces	fl. oz.	30.0	milliliters	ml
cups	c	0.24	liters	l
pints	pt.	0.47	liters	l
quarts	qt.	0.95	liters	l
ounces	oz.	28.0	grams	g
pounds	lb.	0.45	kilograms	kg
Fahrenheit	F	5/9 (after subtracting 32)	Celsius	C

Fahrenheit to Celsius	
F	**C**
200–205	95
229–225	105
245–250	120
275	135
300–305	150
325–330	165
345–350	175
370–375	190
400–405	205
425–430	220
445–450	230
470–475	245
500	260

Liquid Measure to Liters		
1/4 cup	=	0.06 liters
1/2 cup	=	0.12 liters
3/4 cup	=	0.18 liters
1 cup	=	0.24 liters
1-1/4 cup	=	0.30 liters
1-1/2 cup	=	0.36 liters
2 cups	=	0.48 liters
2-1/2 cups	=	0.60 liters
3 cups	=	0.72 liters
3-1/2 cups	=	0.84 liters
4 cups	=	0.96 liters
4-1/2 cups	=	1.08 liters
5 cups	=	1.20 liters
5-1/2 cups	=	1.32 liters

Liquid Measure to Milliliters		
1/4 teaspoon	=	1.25 milliliters
1/2 teaspoon	=	2.50 milliliters
3/4 teaspoon	=	3.75 milliliters
1 teaspoon	=	5.00 milliliters
1-1/4 teaspoons	=	6.25 milliliters
1-1/2 teaspoons	=	7.50 milliliters
1-3/4 teaspoons	=	8.75 milliliters
2 teaspoons	=	10.0 milliliters
1 tablespoon	=	15.0 milliliters
2 tablespoons	=	30.0 milliliters

Index